The best of Mrs BEETON'S Easy Everyday Cooking

The best of Mrs BEETON'S Easy Everyday Cooking

WEIDENFELD & NICOLSON

First published in 2005 by the Orion Publishing Group Ltd
5 Upper St Martin's Lane
London
WC2H 9EA

Text selection © Orion Publishing Group Ltd 2005

Designed by seagulls
Index prepared by Indexing Specialists (UK) Ltd
Produced by Omnipress Ltd, Eastbourne
Printed and bound in the UK by
CPI Mackays, Chatham ME5 8TD

Contents

Soups

Here is a selection of soups for every occasion;
from rib-sticking winter warmers
to chilled soups for hot summer days.
Whether you serve these recipes as starters or
main courses, they are sure to satisfy
even the most jaded palates.

LEEK AND OAT BROTH

1 litre / 1¾ pints pale chicken or vegetable stock
3 leeks, trimmed, sliced and washed
1 bay leaf
salt and pepper
60 ml / 4 tbsp fine or medium oatmeal
150 ml / ¼ pint single cream

Bring the stock and leeks to the boil in a large saucepan. Add the bay leaf and salt and pepper to taste. Lower the heat and simmer for 20 minutes.

Sprinkle the oatmeal into the simmering soup, whisking all the time and simmer for 5 minutes more. Then cover and simmer gently for a further 15–20 minutes, until thickened.

Stir in the cream, reheat without boiling and serve at once.

SERVES FOUR

MRS BEETON'S TIP

*Quick-cook porridge oats may
be substituted for oatmeal and the
soup simmered for just 5 minutes
before adding the cream.*

SOUTHWOLD COD SOUP

25 g / l oz butter
20 ml / 4 tsp olive oil
2 large onions, thinly sliced
1 large carrot, thinly sliced
2 celery sticks, thinly sliced
225 g / 8 oz potatoes, peeled and diced
5 ml / 1 tsp curry powder
1 bouquet garni
salt and pepper
575 g / 1¼ lb cod fillet, skinned and cut into small pieces
45 ml / 3 tbsp white wine (optional)
25 g / l oz cornflour
125 ml / 4 fl oz milk
75 ml / 5 tbsp single cream

Melt the butter in the oil in a deep saucepan. Add the vegetables and fry for 10 minutes.

Stir in the curry powder and cook for 3 minutes. Stir in 750 ml / 1¼ pints boiling water. Add the bouquet garni, with salt and pepper to taste. Add the fish and bring the soup back to simmering point. Cover and simmer for 3–5 minutes until the fish is tender.

Using a slotted spoon, transfer the best pieces of fish to a bowl. Ladle in a little of the soup stock and keep hot.

Reduce the remaining soup by simmering, uncovered, for 15 minutes. Remove the bouquet garni. Rub the soup through a sieve into a clean pan, or process in a blender or food processor. Add the wine, if used, and reheat.

Meanwhile, blend the cornflour with a little of the milk in a bowl. Stir in the rest of the milk. Add the mixture to the soup, stirring constantly. Bring to the boil and cook for 2–3 minutes, stirring constantly. Add the fish, remove the pan from the heat and stir in the cream. Serve at once.

SERVES SIX

FISH BALL SOUP

50 g / 2 oz fresh root ginger, peeled and finely chopped
1 spring onion, finely chopped
15 ml / 1 tbsp dry sherry
1 egg white
225 g / 8 oz firm white fish fillet, skinned and cut into pieces
25 ml / 5 tsp cornflour
salt
25 g / 1 oz lard, softened
snipped chives to garnish

CHINESE CHICKEN STOCK
2 chicken quarters
1 onion, thickly sliced
1 large carrot, thickly sliced
1 celery stick, thickly sliced
1 thin slice of fresh root ginger
5 ml / 1 tsp dry sherry

Make the stock. Put the chicken quarters in a heavy-bottomed saucepan. Add 2 litres / 3½ pints water and bring to the boil. Skim, lower the heat, cover and simmer for 1½ hours. Remove the chicken from the stock and set aside for use in another recipe.

Add the vegetables to the stock, cover and simmer for 20 minutes. Stir in the root ginger and sherry, with salt to taste. Remove the lid and simmer for 10 minutes more. Strain the stock into a clean saucepan, making it up to 1.25 litres / 2½ pints with water if necessary. Skim off any fat on the surface and set aside.

To make the fish balls, sieve the root ginger and spring onion into a bowl containing 75 ml / 5 tbsp water. Stir briskly. Alternatively, process the root ginger, spring onion and water in a blender or food processor. Strain the liquid into a clean bowl, discarding any solids. Add a further 75 ml / 5 tbsp water to the liquid, with the sherry and the egg white. Whisk until smooth.

> ### FREEZER TIP
>
> *The shaped fish balls may be frozen*
> *before cooking. Open freeze them on*
> *a baking sheet lined with freezer*
> *film, then pack in polythene bags*
> *when firm. Cook from frozen in*
> *soup. Alternatively, the fish balls*
> *may be deep fried or stir fried.*

Place the fish in a basin or large mortar and pound it to a paste. Alternatively, purée the fish in a food processor. Transfer 15 ml / 1 tbsp of the sherry mixture to a shallow bowl and add the fish. Stir in the cornflour, salt and lard, and mix thoroughly so that the ingredients bind together. The mixture should be soft and malleable; add more of the sherry mixture as necessary.

Form the fish mixture into balls about 4 cm / 1½ inches in diameter and drop them into a large pan of cold water. Bring the water to the boil, lower the heat and simmer until the fish balls float. Remove with a slotted spoon.

Bring the pan of Chinese chicken stock to the boil. Drop in the fish balls and heat through for 1–2 minutes. Serve immediately, garnished with the chives.

SERVES SIX

SMOKED HADDOCK CHOWDER

450 g / 1 lb smoked haddock fillet, skinned
750 ml / 1¼ pints milk
50 g / 2 oz butter
1 small onion, finely chopped
100 g / 4 oz mushrooms, finely chopped
40 g / 1½ oz plain flour
250 ml / 8 fl oz single cream
freshly-ground black pepper

Put the haddock fillets into a saucepan with the milk and heat to simmering point. Simmer for about 10 minutes until just tender. Drain the fish, reserving the cooking liquid, remove the skin and shred lightly.

Melt the butter in a clean pan, add the onion and mushrooms and fry gently for about 10 minutes until soft. Do not allow the onion to colour.

Stir in the flour and cook for 1 minute, stirring constantly. Gradually add the fish-flavoured milk, stirring until smooth. Bring to the boil, lower the heat and simmer until thickened.

Off the heat, add the cream and the shredded haddock. Return the pan to the heat and warm through gently. Do not allow the soup to boil after adding the cream. Top with a generous grinding of black pepper and serve at once.

SERVES FOUR TO SIX

MRS BEETON'S TIP

Reserve a couple of perfect mushrooms for a garnish. Slice them thinly and sprinkle a few slices on top of each portion of soup. It is not necessary to cook the mushrooms.

SHRIMP AND CIDER BISQUE

*Cooked whole prawns, thawed if frozen, may be used
instead of the shrimps in this bisque.*

750 ml / 1¼ pints fish stock
225 g / 8 oz cooked whole shrimps
45 ml / 3 tbsp fresh white breadcrumbs
50 g / 2oz butter
pinch of grated nutmeg
5 ml / 1 tsp lemon juice
100 ml / 3½ fl oz cider
salt and pepper
1 egg yolk
125 ml / 4 fl oz single cream

Pour the fish stock into a large saucepan. Peel the shrimps and add the shells to the pan. Set the shrimps aside. Bring the stock and shrimp shells to the boil, cover and cook for 10 minutes. Strain into a large measuring jug or heatproof bowl.

Put the breadcrumbs in a small bowl with 250 ml / 8 fl oz of the strained stock. Set aside to soak for 10 minutes.

Meanwhile, melt 25 g / 1 oz of the butter in a pan. Add the shrimps and toss over gentle heat for 5 minutes. Add the nutmeg, lemon juice and breadcrumb mixture and heat gently for 5 minutes. Beat in the rest of the butter.

Purée the mixture in a blender or food processor or rub through a sieve into a clean pan. Gradually add the cider and the remaining stock. Bring to the boil, remove from the heat and add salt and pepper to taste.

In a small bowl, mix the egg yolk with the cream. Stir a little of the hot soup into the egg mixture, mix well, then add the contents of the bowl to the soup, stirring the bisque over low heat until it thickens. Serve at once.

SERVES FOUR TO SIX

CULLEN SKINK

1 large finnan haddock on the bone
1 onion, finely chopped
450 g / 1 lb potatoes, halved
salt and pepper
25 g / 1 oz butter
150 ml / ¼ pint single cream
250 ml / 8 fl oz milk
chopped parsley to garnish

Put the haddock in a large saucepan with the onion. Add 1 litre / 1¾ pints water. Bring to the boil, lower the heat and simmer for 20 minutes. Lift out the fish and remove the skin and bones, returning these to the stock. Flake the fish roughly and set it aside in a clean saucepan. Simmer the stock for a further 45 minutes until flavoursome.

Meanwhile cook the potatoes in a saucepan of lightly salted water for about 30 minutes or until tender. Drain thoroughly and mash with the butter.

Strain the fish stock into the pan containing the flaked fish. Set aside 60 ml / 4 tbsp of the cream in a small jug. Add the remaining cream to the pan with the milk. Stir in the mashed potato and heat through, stirring to make a thick soup. If a thinner soup is preferred, add more milk.

Check the seasoning. The soup is unlikely to need salt, but pepper may be added, if liked. Ladle into individual bowls, drizzling a little of the reserved cream on to the surface of each portion. Sprinkle with chopped parsley and serve at once.

SERVES FOUR

BORSCH

30 ml / 2 tbsp oil
1 onion, roughly chopped
1 garlic clove, sliced
1 carrot, sliced
1 turnip, sliced
1 swede, sliced
2 tomatoes, peeled and chopped
350 g / 12 oz raw beetroot, grated
1 bay leaf
2 litres / 3½ pints strong stock
30 ml / 2 tbsp tomato purée
salt and pepper
225 g / 8 oz cabbage, sliced
225 g / 8 oz potatoes, cubed
5 ml / 1 tsp cider vinegar
150 ml / ¼ pint soured cream
chopped dill to garnish

Heat the oil in a large saucepan. Add the onion, garlic, carrot, turnip and swede and cook for 10 minutes, stirring frequently to prevent the vegetables from sticking to the base of the pan. Stir in the tomatoes and beetroot, with the bay leaf. Add the stock and tomato purée, with salt and pepper to taste. Bring to the boil, lower the heat, cover and simmer for 1 hour.

Add the sliced cabbage and cubed potato. Stir in the vinegar and simmer for 15 minutes more or until the potato cubes are tender. Taste the soup and add more salt and pepper, if required.

Leave to stand for 5 minutes. Serve topped with soured cream and garnished with dill.

SERVES SIX

COCK-A-LEEKIE

100 g / 4 oz prunes
450 g / 1 lb leeks, trimmed, sliced and washed
1 (1.4 kg / 3 lb) chicken
3 rindless streaky bacon rashers, chopped
2.5 ml / ½ tsp salt
1 bouquet garni
1.25 ml / ¼ tsp pepper

Soak the prunes overnight in a small bowl of water, then drain them and remove the stones. Set aside, with about one-third of the drained leek slices.

Put the chicken, with its giblets if available, and bacon in a deep saucepan. Add cold water to cover (about 2 litres / 3½ pints). Stir in the salt and bring slowly to simmering point.

Add the remaining leeks to the pan, with the bouquet garni and pepper. Cover, then simmer gently for about 3 hours or until the chicken is cooked through and tender.

Carefully remove the chicken, discard the skin, then carve off the meat and cut it into fairly large serving pieces. Return the chicken meat to the soup and add the reserved prunes and leeks. Simmer gently for about 30 minutes, until the prunes are cooked but not broken. Skim off surface fat and check seasoning before serving.

SERVES SIX TO EIGHT

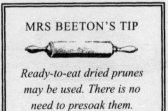

MRS BEETON'S TIP

Ready-to-eat dried prunes may be used. There is no need to presoak them.

SCOTCH BROTH

This economical soup was originally intended to furnish two meals:
the meat was removed after cooking and served separately.
Today it is more usual to cut up the meat and add it to the soup.

25 g / 1 oz pearl barley
450 g / 1 lb middle neck of lamb, trimmed of excess fat
1.4 litres / 2½ pints pale chicken or vegetable stock
1 onion, chopped
1 leek, trimmed, sliced and washed
2 carrots, sliced
1 swede, cubed
salt and pepper

Put the barley in a small saucepan with water to cover. Bring to the boil, then drain off the water and transfer the barley to a large pan with the meat and stock. Bring the mixture to the boil, skim off any scum on the surface, then lower the heat and simmer gently for 2 hours.

Add the vegetables with plenty of salt and pepper. Simmer for a further 45–60 minutes. Lift out the meat, remove it from the bones, and roughly chop it. Skim off any fat from the broth, add more salt and pepper if required, then replace the chopped meat. Serve very hot.

SERVES FOUR

MRS BEETON'S MULLIGATAWNY

25 g / 1 oz butter
30 ml / 2 tbsp oil
1 chicken, skinned and jointed or 900 g / 2 lb chicken portions
4 rindless back bacon rashers, chopped
3 onions, sliced
1 garlic clove, crushed
15 ml / 1 tbsp mild curry powder
25 g / 1 oz ground almonds
2 litres / 3½ pints chicken stock
175 g / 6 oz red lentils
salt and pepper
hot boiled rice to serve

Heat the butter and oil in a large, heavy-bottomed saucepan. Add the chicken and brown the joints all over, then remove them from the pan and set aside. Add the bacon, onions and garlic to the fat remaining in the pan and cook over gentle heat for 5 minutes, then stir in the curry powder and cook for 2 minutes more.

In a small bowl, mix the ground almonds to a paste with a little of the stock. Set aside. Add the remaining stock to the pan and return the chicken joints. Bring to the boil, lower the heat and simmer for 1 hour or until the chicken is tender.

Remove the chicken and cut the meat off the bones, then set aside. Skim any fat off the soup. Add the lentils and bring back to the boil. Reduce the heat, cover and simmer the soup for 30 minutes.

Stir the almond paste into the pan and replace the chicken meat. Simmer for a further 5–10 minutes. Taste for seasoning before serving very hot, with boiled rice.

SERVES EIGHT

CREAMY ONION SOUP

50 g / 2 oz butter
4 large onions, finely chopped
50 g / 2 oz plain flour
1.1 litres / 2 pints pale chicken or vegetable stock
salt and white pepper
1.25 ml / ¼ tsp ground mace
2 egg yolks
150 ml / ¼ pint double cream

Melt the butter in the top of a double saucepan. Add the onions and cook over gentle heat for 10 minutes until soft but not coloured.

Stir in the flour and cook for 1 minute, then gradually add the stock. Cook over moderate heat until the mixture boils and thickens. Season to taste with salt, pepper and mace.

Set the pan over simmering water and cook the soup, stirring occasionally, for about 30 minutes or until the onions are very tender and the soup is creamy.

In a small bowl, mix the egg yolks with the cream. Stir a little of the hot soup into the egg mixture, mix well, then add the contents of the bowl to the soup, stirring over the simmering water until it thickens. Serve at once.

SERVES FOUR TO SIX

SOUP A LA CRECY

*This soup is extremely tasty and quite filling
if served with the addition of rice.*

salt and pepper
100 g / 4 oz long-grain rice (optional)
50 g / 2 oz butter
4 carrots, sliced
2 onions, thinly sliced
100 g / 4 oz red lentils
1.75 litres / 3 pints chicken stock
1 lettuce, shredded
50 g / 2 oz fresh white breadcrumbs

If using the rice, bring a saucepan of salted water to the boil. Add the rice and cook for 12 minutes. Drain thoroughly, rinse under cold water and drain again. Set aside.

Melt the butter in a large saucepan, add the carrots and onions and fry over gentle heat for about 10 minutes until soft. Stir in the lentils, turning them in the butter, then add the stock. Bring to the boil, lower the heat and simmer for 20 minutes, stirring occasionally.

Stir in the lettuce and breadcrumbs, with plenty of salt and pepper. Simmer for 10 minutes more. Purée the soup in a blender or food processor, or rub through a sieve into a clean pan. Reheat with the rice if using and serve.

SERVES EIGHT

PARSNIP SOUP

25 g / 1 oz butter
1 onion, chopped
450 g / 1 lb parsnips, sliced
1 litre / 1¾ pints chicken stock or vegetable stock
salt and cayenne pepper
150 ml / ¼ pint single cream
30 ml / 2 tbsp pine nuts (optional)

Melt the butter in a large saucepan, add the onion and parsnips, and cook over gentle heat for 10 minutes, turning frequently to coat them in the butter.

Add the stock, with salt and cayenne pepper to taste. Bring to the boil, lower the heat and simmer for 20 minutes until the parsnips are very soft.

Purée the soup in a blender or food processor, or rub through a sieve into a clean pan. Reheat it to just below boiling point, then stir in most of the cream, reserving about 30 ml / 2 tbsp for the garnish.

Meanwhile spread out the pine nuts (if used) in a grill pan and toast them under a hot grill until golden. Ladle the soup into individual bowls and top each portion with a swirl of cream and a sprinkling of toasted pine nuts.

SERVES FOUR

VARIATION

- **Spiced Parsnip Soup** Add 5 ml / 1 tsp good-quality curry powder to the onion and parsnips when cooking in the butter. Substitute plain yogurt for the cream and use roughly chopped cashew nuts instead of the pine nuts. Sprinkle with a little chopped fresh coriander leaves, if liked.

CHANTILLY SOUP

Use fresh young peas to make this simple soup. The best pods
are plump and well filled without being too tightly packed.

30 ml / 2 tbsp butter
2 onions, finely chopped
1.4 kg / 3 lb peas in the pod (about 675 g / 1½ lb when shelled)
1 small bunch of parsley, chopped
1.5 litres / 2¾ pints chicken stock
salt and pepper

Melt the butter in a large saucepan. Add the onions and cook over gentle heat for 10 minutes until soft but not coloured.

Meanwhile shell the peas, reserving about 6 of the best pods. Stir the peas and parsley into the pan and add the stock, with salt and pepper to taste. Wash the pods and add them to the pan.

Bring the stock to simmering point (see Mrs Beeton's Tip) and cook for about 20 minutes, or until the peas are very soft. Remove the pods.

Purée the soup in a blender or food processor, or rub through a sieve into a clean pan. Bring to just below boiling point and serve at once.

SERVES SIX

MRS BEETON'S TIP

Do not allow the soup to
boil after the peas have
been added, or you will
spoil the colour.

CABBAGE SOUP

*Cabbage and bacon go wonderfully well together,
a fact that is celebrated in this hearty soup.*

15 ml / 1 tbsp oil
175 g / 6 oz rindless streaky bacon rashers
2 carrots, thinly sliced
1 large onion, thinly sliced
1 large cabbage, shredded
1. 1 litres / 2 pints pale chicken or vegetable stock
pepper to taste
croûtons to serve (optional)

Heat the oil in a large heavy-bottomed saucepan or flameproof casserole. Add the bacon and cook, stirring, for 5 minutes. Add the carrots and onion, then cook gently for 10 minutes. Stir in the cabbage and add the stock. Bring to the boil, lower the heat and cover the pan. Simmer for 45 minutes, until the vegetables are tender and the soup well flavoured.

Taste the soup for seasoning and add pepper. The bacon usually makes the soup sufficiently salty, depending on the stock. Skim off any excess surface fat, then serve the soup very hot, with croûtons, if liked.

SERVES EIGHT

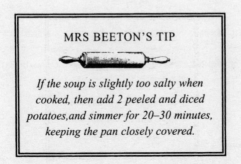

MRS BEETON'S TIP

*If the soup is slightly too salty when
cooked, then add 2 peeled and diced
potatoes, and simmer for 20–30 minutes,
keeping the pan closely covered.*

CARROT SOUP

Grating the vegetables speeds up the cooking time considerably, making this an ideal soup for those occasions when time is short.

600 ml / 1 pint chicken stock or vegetable stock
3 carrots, grated
1 onion, finely chopped
1 potato, grated
25 g / 1 oz butter
25 g / 1 oz plain flour
300 ml / ½ pint milk
salt and pepper
grated nutmeg

Combine the stock, carrots, onion and potato in a saucepan. Bring to the boil, lower the heat and simmer for about 15 minutes or until the vegetables are tender.

Meanwhile melt the butter in a separate saucepan, add the flour and cook for 1 minute. Gradually stir in the milk, then add the stock and vegetables. Heat, stirring constantly, until the mixture boils and thickens. Add salt, pepper and nutmeg to taste. Serve at once, with triangles of hot toast, if liked.

SERVES FOUR

VARIATION

• **Carrot and Orange Soup** Cut the carrot into matchstick strips and use a parsnip, cut into similar strips, instead of the potato. Use 900 ml / 1½ pints stock and add 60 ml / 4 tbsp fresh orange juice. Omit the milk and do not thicken the soup.

CREAM OF TOMATO SOUP

25 g / 1 oz butter
2 rindless back bacon rashers, chopped
1 small onion, chopped
1 carrot, chopped
900 g / 2 lb tomatoes, chopped
600 ml / 1 pint pale chicken or vegetable stock
1 bouquet garni
salt and pepper
10 ml / 2 tsp sugar
300 ml / ½ pint double cream
chopped parsley or snipped chives to garnish

Melt the butter in a large saucepan, add the bacon and fry for 2–3 minutes. Stir in the onion and carrot and fry over gentle heat for 5 minutes, then add the tomatoes and cook for 5 minutes more.

Add the stock and bouquet garni, with salt and pepper to taste. Bring to the boil, lower the heat and simmer for about 20 minutes, until the vegetables are soft.

Remove the bouquet garni. Purée the soup in a blender or food processor, then rub through a sieve to remove traces of skin and seeds.

Return the soup to the rinsed-out pan. Stir in the sugar and reheat to just below boiling point. Stir in the cream, heat briefly but do not allow to simmer or the soup will curdle. Taste and adjust the seasoning, then serve at once, topped with chopped parsley or snipped chives.

SERVES SIX

CAULIFLOWER SOUP

1 large cauliflower
25 g / 1 oz butter
1 onion, finely chopped
900 ml / 1½ pints milk
salt and pepper
2 egg yolks
150 ml / ¼ pint single cream
50 g / 2 oz flaked almonds, toasted

Steam the cauliflower whole for 20–30 minutes until tender. Cut it into florets, reserving any leaves or tender stems.

Melt the butter in a small frying pan. Add the onion and cook over gentle heat for about 10 minutes, until soft but not coloured. Purée the cauliflower and the onion mixture with 250 ml / 8 fl oz of the milk in a blender or food processor, then rub through a fine sieve into a clean pan.

Stir the remaining milk into the pan, with salt and pepper to taste. Heat the soup to just below boiling point, then lower the heat so that it barely simmers. In a small bowl, mix the egg yolks with the cream. Stir a little of the hot soup into the egg mixture, mix well, then add the contents of the bowl to the soup, stirring over low heat until it thickens. Serve at once, topping each portion with toasted almonds.

SERVES FOUR

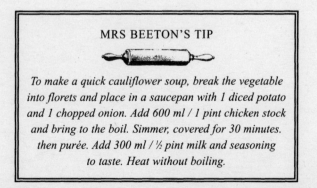

MRS BEETON'S TIP

To make a quick cauliflower soup, break the vegetable into florets and place in a saucepan with 1 diced potato and 1 chopped onion. Add 600 ml / 1 pint chicken stock and bring to the boil. Simmer, covered for 30 minutes. then purée. Add 300 ml / ½ pint milk and seasoning to taste. Heat without boiling.

YELLOW SPLIT PEA SOUP

30 ml / 2 tbsp oil
6 rindless streaky bacon rashers, chopped
1 large onion, finely chopped
100 g / 4 oz yellow split peas, soaked overnight in water to cover
2 litres / 3½ pints chicken stock or vegetable stock
60 ml / 4 tbsp chopped celery leaves
2 parsley sprigs & 2 bay leaves
5 ml / 1 tsp chopped summer savory or 2.5 ml / ½ tsp dried savory
salt and pepper

Heat the oil in a large saucepan. Add the bacon and onion. Fry for 10 minutes over gentle heat, until the onion is soft but not coloured.

Drain the split peas and add them to the pan with the stock, celery leaves, parsley, bay leaves and savory. Add salt and pepper to taste. Bring to the boil, lower the heat and simmer for about 2 hours, or until the peas are very tender. If the soup becomes too thick, add water or extra stock.

Remove the parsley sprigs and bay leaves. Serve the soup as it is, or purée in a blender or food processor. Alternatively, rub through a sieve into a clean pan. Reheat, stirring frequently to prevent the soup from sticking to the pan, and serve at once.

SERVES FOUR TO SIX

BEAN SOUP

The perfect warmer for a chilly winter's night, this soup is a meal in itself.

450 g / 1 lb haricot beans, soaked overnight in water to cover
100 g / 4 oz fat bacon, diced
2 onions, sliced
10 ml / 2 tsp dried thyme
salt and pepper
15 ml / 1 tbsp chopped parsley

Drain the beans. Put them in a large heavy-bottomed saucepan. Add 2.25 litres / 4 pints water and bring to the boil. Boil vigorously for 10 minutes, then lower the heat and simmer for 45 minutes or until the beans are almost tender. Drain, reserving the bean stock.

Put the bacon in the clean pan and heat gently until the fat runs. Add the onions and fry over moderate heat for 3–4 minutes. Stir in the beans with the thyme. Add the reserved bean stock, with salt and pepper to taste. Simmer for 1 hour, stirring occasionally to prevent the soup from sticking to the pan.

Check the seasoning and add more salt and pepper if required. Stir in the parsley and serve at once, with chunks of wholemeal bread.

SERVES SIX TO EIGHT

VARIATIONS

- **Two-bean Soup** Use half red kidney beans instead of haricot beans alone. Add 1 diced green pepper with the onions.
- **Vegetarian Bean Soup** Omit the bacon and fry the onion in 25 g / 1 oz butter with 1 crushed garlic clove. Stir in 45 ml / 3 tbsp tahini with the parsley.

FRESH ASPARAGUS SOUP

450 g / 1 lb fresh asparagus
salt and white pepper
1.4 litres / 2 pints chicken stock
50 g / 2 oz butter
1 small onion, chopped
50 g / 2 oz plain flour
1 egg yolk
150 ml / 1 pint double cream

Cut off the asparagus tips and put them in a saucepan. Add salted water to cover, bring to the boil, then simmer for about 5 minutes or until tender. Drain and set aside.

Slice the asparagus stalks and cook them in 600 ml / 1 pint of the stock for about 15 minutes or until tender. Purée in a blender or food processor, or rub through a sieve into a bowl or large jug.

Melt the butter in a large saucepan, add the onion and fry over gentle heat for about 10 minutes until soft but not coloured. Stir in the flour and cook for 1 minute, stirring constantly.

Gradually add the remaining stock, stirring until the mixture boils and thickens. Stir in the asparagus purée, with salt and pepper to taste. Reheat.

In a small bowl, mix the egg yolk with the cream. Stir a little of the hot soup into the egg mixture, mix well, then add the contents of the bowl to the soup, stirring over low heat until the mixture thickens slightly. Add the reserved asparagus tips and heat through without boiling. Serve at once.

SERVES SIX

SPINACH SOUP

25 g / 1 oz butter
1 large onion, finely chopped
1. 1 litres / 2 pints chicken stock
2 potatoes, diced
900 g / 2 lb spinach, washed, trimmed and roughly chopped
2.5 ml / ½ tsp grated nutmeg
salt and pepper
150 ml / ¼ pint single cream
2 rindless back bacon rashers, grilled and crumbled, to garnish (optional)

Melt the butter, add the onion and cook over gentle heat for 10 minutes until soft but not coloured. Add the stock and potatoes and cook for 15 minutes.

Add the spinach and cook for 10 minutes more or until both potatoes and spinach are tender. Purée the soup in a blender or food processor, or rub through a sieve into a clean pan. Add the nutmeg, with salt and pepper to taste.

Stir in the cream and reheat without boiling. Serve the soup in individual bowls, topping each portion with crumbled bacon, if liked.

SERVES FOUR

VARIATION

- **Green and Gold** Fry the onion in the butter as described above. Meanwhile cook the spinach with just the water that clings to the leaves after washing. Drain thoroughly, pressing the spinach against the sides of the colander with a wooden spoon to extract as much liquid as possible, then mix the spinach with the onion mixture. Form into egg-sized balls. Bring the stock to the boil. Spoon a few spinach balls into each soup bowl, add the boiling stock and serve at once.

CREAM OF ALMOND SOUP

*The delicate flavour of this soup makes it the perfect
introduction to a simple summer meal.*

300 ml / ½ pint milk
175 ml / 6 fl oz single cream
pared rind of 1 lemon
50 g / 2 oz butter
50 g / 2 oz plain flour
1 litre / 1¾ pints chicken stock
salt and pepper
75 g / 3 oz ground almonds
pinch of cayenne pepper
2.5 ml / ½ tsp ground mace

Combine the milk, cream and lemon rind in a saucepan. Bring to just below
boiling point, then remove from the heat.

Melt the butter in the top of a double saucepan, stir in the flour and cook for
2 minutes. Gradually add the stock, stirring all the time until the mixture boils
and thickens. Add salt and pepper to taste.

Remove from the heat. Gradually stir in the milk mixture. When the mixture is
smooth and creamy, add the ground almonds, cayenne and mace. Place the pan
over simmering water and cook for 15 minutes, stirring frequently. Remove the
lemon rind and serve.

SERVES FOUR TO SIX

CUCUMBER AND YOGURT SOUP

Low in calories, this is the ideal soup for a summer lunch party.

15 ml / 1 tbsp butter or light olive oil
1 small onion, finely chopped
½ large cucumber, peeled and cut into 5 mm / 1 inch dice
450 ml / ¾ pint plain yogurt
250 ml / 8 fl oz chicken or well-flavoured
vegetable stock
grated rind and juice of lemon
10 ml / 2 tsp finely chopped mint
salt and pepper
mint sprigs to garnish

Melt the butter in a saucepan, add the onion and cucumber and cook over very gentle heat for 8–10 minutes. Leave to cool.

Whisk the yogurt in a bowl until smooth. Add the onion mixture with the stock. Stir in the lemon rind and juice, with the mint. Add salt and pepper to taste. Cover the bowl and chill for several hours. Serve in chilled bowls, garnished with mint sprigs.

SERVES THREE TO FOUR

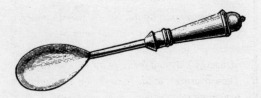

VICHYSOISSE

A simple soup which can be served hot, but tastes even better chilled.

25 g / 1 oz butter
450 g / 1 lb leeks, white parts only, trimmed, sliced and washed
2 onions, chopped
450 g / 1 lb potatoes, cubed
900 ml / 1½ pints chicken stock
salt and pepper
150 ml / ¼ pint milk
150 ml / ¼ pint single cream
snipped chives to garnish

Melt the butter in a saucepan, add the leeks, onions and potatoes and fry gently for 10 minutes without browning. Stir in the stock, with salt and pepper to taste. Bring to the boil, lower the heat and simmer for about 30 minutes or until the vegetables are soft.

Purée the mixture in a blender or food processor, or press through a sieve into a bowl. Cool quickly, then stir in the milk and cream. Add more salt and pepper if required. Cover and chill for 4–6 hours. Serve in chilled individual bowls, sprinkled with chives.

SERVES FOUR TO SIX

FREEZER TIP

Make the soup as above, but use only 1 onion and 600 ml / 1 pint chicken stock. After puréeing the vegetables and stock, cool the mixture quickly and freeze in a rigid container. Thaw overnight in the refrigerator. Stir in the remaining stock with the milk and cream, then chill for at least 2 hours more before serving.

GAZPACHO

2 thick slices of bread, cubed
1 litre / 1¾ pints tomato juice
1 small onion, finely chopped
2 garlic cloves, crushed
1 cucumber, finely chopped
1 green pepper, seeded and chopped
6 tomatoes, peeled and chopped
75 ml / 3 fl oz olive oil
30 ml / 2 tbsp red wine vinegar
1.25 ml / ¼ tsp dried oregano
1.25 ml / ¼ tsp dried mixed herbs
salt and pepper

TO SERVE
croûtons (see Mrs Beeton's Tip, below)
diced cucumber
diced onion
black olives

Put the bread cubes in a large bowl with the tomato juice. Leave to soak for 5 minutes, then add the chopped vegetables. Stir in the olive oil, cover and leave to stand for 1 hour.

Purée the soup in a blender or food processor, then rub through a sieve into a clean bowl. Stir in the vinegar and herbs, with salt and pepper to taste. Cover the bowl closely and chill for 2–3 hours. Serve with the suggested accompaniments, in separate bowls.

SERVES FOUR

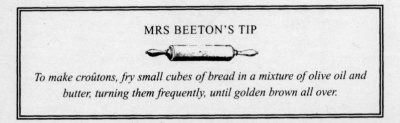

MRS BEETON'S TIP

To make croûtons, fry small cubes of bread in a mixture of olive oil and butter, turning them frequently, until golden brown all over.

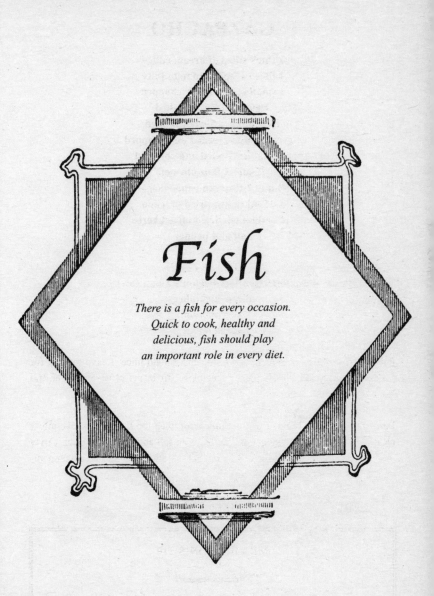

Fish

There is a fish for every occasion.
Quick to cook, healthy and
delicious, fish should play
an important role in every diet.

COURT BOUILLON

This is the traditional cooking liquid for poached fish. The flavours infuse and enhance the fish, and the liquor is discarded after use.

500 ml / 17 fl oz dry white wine or dry cider
30 ml / 2 tbsp white wine vinegar
2 large carrots, sliced
2 large onions, sliced
2–3 celery sticks, chopped
6 parsley stalks. crushed
1 bouquet garni
10 peppercorns, lightly crushed
salt and pepper

Put the wine in a large stainless steel or enamel saucepan. Add 1 litre / 1¾ pints water, with the remaining ingredients. Bring to the boil, lower the heat and simmer for 30 minutes. Cool, then strain and use as required.

MAKES 1.5 LITRES / 2¾ PINTS

COD WITH CREAM SAUCE

6 (100 g / 4 oz) cod steaks or portions
75 g / 3 oz butter
250 ml / 8 fl oz pale fish stock
milk (see method)
25 g / 1 oz plain flour
30 ml / 2 tbsp double cream
15 ml / 1 tbsp lemon juice
salt and pepper

Rinse the fish and pat dry on absorbent kitchen paper. Melt half the butter in a frying pan, add the cod and fry quickly on both sides to seal without browning.

Add the stock, cover the pan and simmer gently for 20 minutes. Drain the fish, reserving the cooking liquid in a measuring jug, place on a warmed dish and keep hot. Make the cooking liquid up to 300 ml / ½ pint with milk.

Melt the remaining butter in a saucepan, add the flour and cook for 1 minute, stirring. Gradually add the reserved cooking liquid and milk mixture, stirring constantly. Bring to the boil, lower the heat and simmer for 4 minutes, stirring occasionally.

Remove the pan from the heat and stir in the cream and lemon juice. Add salt and pepper to taste and spoon a little sauce over each fish portion. Serve at once.

SERVES SIX

FISH PUDDING

This old-fashioned pudding is light and delicately flavoured, rather similar to fish cakes made with breadcrumbs rather than potato.

fat for greasing
450 g / 1 lb white fish fillet (cod, haddock, hake or ling),
skinned and finely chopped
50 g / 2 oz shredded suet
50 g / 2 oz fresh white breadcrumbs
30 ml / 2 tbsp chopped parsley
salt and pepper
few drops of anchovy essence
2 eggs, lightly beaten
125 ml / 4 fl oz milk
lemon wedges to serve

Grease a 1.1 litre / 2 pint pudding basin. Prepare a steamer or half fill a large saucepan with water and bring to the boil.

Combine the fish, suet, breadcrumbs and parsley in a bowl. Mix well and add salt, pepper and anchovy essence.

Stir in the eggs and milk. Spoon the mixture into the prepared basin, cover with greased greaseproof paper or foil and secure with string.

Put the pudding in the perforated part of the steamer, or stand it on an old saucer or plate in the saucepan of boiling water. The water should come halfway up the sides of the basin. Cover the pan tightly and steam the pudding for 1½ hours.

Leave for 5–10 minutes at room temperature to firm up, then turn out on to a warmed serving plate. Serve with a parsley or mushroom sauce, if liked, or with lemon wedges for their juice.

SERVES FOUR

PLAICE WITH GINGER

25 g / 1 oz butter
2 onions, sliced
8 plaice fillets, skinned and cut into 5 cm / 2 inch wide strips
salt and pepper
15 ml / 1 tbsp ground ginger
juice of 3 lemons
4 eggs, beaten

Melt the butter in a large frying pan, add the onions and cook until lightly browned. Add the fish, salt, pepper, ginger, lemon juice and 150 ml / ¼ pint water. Heat until simmering, cover and cook gently for 20 minutes. Transfer the fish to a serving dish and keep hot.

Slowly beat the cooking liquor into the eggs. Pour the mixture back into the pan and cook gently, whisking all the time, until the eggs are creamy. Do not over-cook or stop whisking. Pour over the fish and serve.

SERVES FOUR

RED MULLET WITH TOMATOES & OLIVES

150 ml / ¼ pint olive oil
1 onion, finely chopped
1 garlic clove, crushed
25 g / 1 oz parsley, chopped
225 g / 8 oz tomatoes, peeled, seeded and chopped
5 ml / 1 tsp tomato purée
salt and pepper
1 bouquet garni
4 (225 g / 8 oz) red mullet, cleaned and scaled
8 black olives, stoned
75 ml / 5 tbsp dry white wine
lemon slices, to garnish

Heat 100 ml / 3½ fl oz of the olive oil in a saucepan, add the onion and fry for 3–4 minutes until lightly browned. Add the garlic and parsley, with the chopped tomatoes. Stir in the tomato purée, with salt and pepper to taste, and add the bouquet garni. Simmer for 15 minutes.

Heat the remaining oil in a deep frying pan and fry the fish gently for 5 minutes, turning once.

When the sauce is cooked, remove the bouquet garni and add the olives and wine. Drain the excess oil from the frying pan. Pour the sauce over the fish, cover the pan and cook for 10 minutes more.

Carefully transfer the fish and sauce to a warmed serving dish. Serve at once, garnished with lemon slices.

SERVES FOUR

SCALLOPED HADDOCK

fat for greasing
450 g / 1 lb potatoes, halved and cooked
salt and pepper
75 g / 3 oz butter
15–30 ml / 1–2 tbsp single cream
250 ml / 8 fl oz milk
30 ml / 2 tbsp chopped onion
1 blade of mace
225 g / 8 oz smoked haddock
25 g / 1 oz plain flour
30 ml / 2 tbsp chopped parsley
30 ml / 2 tbsp double cream
browned breadcrumbs

Grease 4 shallow, individual ovenproof dishes. Set the oven at 200°C / 400°F / gas 6. Mash the potatoes until smooth. Beat in 25 g / 1 oz of the butter and the single cream.

Combine the milk, onion and mace in a deep frying pan. Bring to simmering point, add the fish and poach gently for 5–8 minutes. Using a slotted spoon, transfer the fish to a large plate. Remove any skin and flake the fish, then divide it between the dishes. Reserve the cooking liquid.

Melt half the remaining butter in a saucepan, add the flour and cook for 1 minute, stirring. Gradually add the reserved cooking liquid and boil, stirring. Add seasoning, parsley and double cream. Pour the sauce over the fish. Sprinkle with the breadcrumbs.

Spoon the creamed potato into a piping bag fitted with a large star nozzle and pipe a border of mashed potato around the edge of each dish. Stand the dishes on a large baking sheet and bake for 4–5 minutes until browned.

SERVES FOUR

HAM AND HADDIE

125 ml / 4 fl oz milk
575 g / 1¼ lb finnan haddock on the bone
25 g / 1 oz butter
4 (100 g / 4 oz) slices of cooked ham
pepper
45 ml / 3 tbsp double cream

Pour the milk into a large frying pan. Heat to just below boiling point, add the haddock, lower the heat and simmer for 10–15 minutes or until the fish is cooked.

Using a slotted spoon and a fish slice, transfer the fish to a large plate. Remove the skin and bones from the fish and flake the flesh. Reserve the cooking liquid in a jug.

Melt the butter in a clean frying pan and add the ham slices. Heat through, turning once, then arrange the ham slices in a warmed flameproof dish. Spoon the flaked fish over the ham and pour the reserved cooking liquid over. Add pepper to taste, then drizzle the cream over the dish. Brown quickly under a hot grill.

SERVES FOUR

JUGGED HADDOCK

4 pieces of finnan haddock fillet
2 bay leaves
4 thyme sprigs
4 parsley sprigs
75 g / 3 oz butter, melted
freshly-ground black pepper

Rinse a heatproof bowl with boiling water to heat it. Lay the fish and herbs in the dish, then pour in boiling water to cover. Cover and leave for 10 minutes. Drain the haddock and serve with hot melted butter and pepper.

SERVES FOUR

SKATE IN BLACK BUTTER

1–2 skate wings, total weight about 800 g / 1¼ lb
1 litre / 1¾ pints court bouillon (page 30)
25 g / 1 oz butter
salt and pepper
30 ml / 2 tbsp capers
30 ml / 2 tsp chopped parsley
75 ml / 5 tbsp wine vinegar

Rinse and dry the skate and cut it into serving portions. Put the fish in a deep frying pan and cover with court bouillon. Bring to simmering point and simmer for 15–20 minutes or until the fish is cooked.

Using a slotted spoon and a fish slice, lift out the fish and transfer to a platter or board. Scrape away the skin. Place the fish in a warmed ovenproof dish and keep hot.

Pour off the court bouillon from the frying pan, add the butter to the pan and heat until it is a rich golden brown. Spoon over the fish, sprinkle with salt and pepper to taste and scatter the capers and parsley over the top. Pour the vinegar into the pan, swill it around while heating quickly, then pour it over the fish. Serve at once.

SERVES THREE TO FOUR

VARIATION

- **Skate with Caper Sauce** Cook and skin the skate as above. Meanwhile, cut 30 ml / 2 tbsp capers into quarters and mix them with 5 ml / 1 tsp of the vinegar from the jar. Cut 100 g / 4 oz butter into chunks and place in a small saucepan. Sprinkle 10 ml / 2 tsp plain flour and 150 ml / ¼ pint water over the butter. Stir steadily in the same direction over medium heat until the butter melts. Bring to the boil and remove from the heat. Stir in the capers, 15 ml / 1 tbsp anchovy essence and pepper to taste. Pour over the skate.

TWEED KETTLE

575 g / 1¼ lb middle cut salmon
500 g / 17 fl oz fish stock
250 ml / 8 fl oz dry white wine
pinch of ground mace
salt and pepper
25 g / 1 oz chopped shallots or snipped chives
5 ml / 1 tsp chopped parsley
25 g / 1 oz butter
30 ml / 2 tbsp plain flour

Put the salmon in a saucepan with the fish stock, wine and mace. Add salt and pepper to taste. Bring the liquid to simmering point and simmer gently for 10–15 minutes or until the fish is just cooked through.

Using a slotted spoon and a fish slice, transfer the fish to a large plate. Remove the skin and bones and return them to the stock in the pan. Transfer the skinned fish to a warmed serving dish and keep hot.

Simmer the stock and fish trimmings for 10 minutes, then strain into a clean pan. Simmer gently, uncovered, until reduced by half. Stir in the shallots or chives and the parsley and remove from the heat.

In a small bowl, blend the butter with the flour. Gradually add small pieces of the mixture to the stock, whisking thoroughly after each addition. Return to the heat and simmer for 5 minutes, stirring. Pour the sauce over the fish and serve at once.

SERVES FOUR

PRAWN CELESTE

50 g / 2 oz butter
100 g / 4 oz mushrooms, sliced
15 ml / 1 tbsp plain flour
salt and pepper
125 ml / 4 fl oz milk
125 ml / 4 fl oz single cream
225 g / 8 oz peeled cooked prawns
15 ml / 1 tbsp dry sherry
chopped parsley, to garnish
4 slices of toast, cut in triangles, to serve

Melt the butter in a saucepan, add the mushrooms and cook over moderate heat for 3–4 minutes. Stir in the flour, with salt and pepper to taste and cook gently for 3 minutes. Gradually add the milk and cream, stirring constantly until the sauce thickens. Add the prawns and sherry. Spoon into a warmed serving dish, garnish with the chopped parsley and serve with the toast triangles.

SERVES FOUR

HOT POACHED SALMON

Serve hot poached salmon with Hollandaise Sauce (page 231).
Cold poached salmon may be garnished with cucumber slices.
See Garnishing Salmon, page 42.

1 (1.6–3.25 kg / 3½–7 lb) salmon
about 3.5 litres / 6 pints Court Bouillon (page 30)

Cut the fins from the fish, remove the scales and thoroughly wash the body cavity. Tie the mouth of the fish shut. Tie the body of the fish loosely to keep it in shape during cooking – two or three bands of string around the fish to prevent the body cavity from gaping are usually sufficient. Weigh the fish and calculate the cooking time. Allow 5 minutes per 450 g / 1 lb for salmon up to 2.25 kg / 5 lb in weight; 4 minutes per 450 g / 1 lb plus 5 minutes for salmon up to 3.25 kg / 7 lb.

Put the fish in a fish kettle and pour over the court bouillon. Bring the liquid gently to just below boiling point. Lower the heat and simmer for the required cooking time. The court bouillon should barely show signs of simmering; if the liquid is allowed to bubble then it may damage the delicate salmon flesh. If serving the salmon cold, simmer for 5 minutes only, then leave the fish to cool in the cooking liquid.

MICROWAVE TIP

Provided it can be curled into a circular dish that will fit into your microwave, salmon may be cooked by this method. Prepare the fish, tuck 2 bay leaves, some peppercorns and a small sprig of parsley into the body cavity, then curl the fish into the dish (a 25 cm / 10 inch quiche dish works well). Cover fish and dish with two layers of microwave-proof film to hold the fish securely and prevent it from losing its shape. Cook on High. A 2.25 kg / 5 lb salmon will take about 12 minutes. If you do not have a turntable turn the dish three times while cooking. Allow to stand, covered, for 5 minutes. To serve hot, drain, remove the herbs from the body cavity and skin as suggested above. Allow to cool in the wrapping if serving cold.

Drain the salmon well and untie the body. Slide the salmon on to a large, heated platter. Slit the skin around the body immediately below the head and just above the tail of the fish. Carefully peel back the skin from the head towards the tail. Carefully turn the fish over and remove the skin from the second side. Untie the mouth.

Garnish the salmon with lemon slices and parsley sprigs. Freshly cooked vegetables (new potatoes and baby carrots) may be arranged around the fish. Serve at once.

SERVINGS FROM SALMON

Hot salmon served as a main course will yield the servings below. If the fish is served cold and dressed, as part of a buffet with other main dishes, then it will yield about 2 extra portions.

1.6 kg / 3½ lb salmon – 4 portions
2.25 kg / 5 lb salmon – 6 portions
3.25 kg / 7 lb salmon – 10 portions

DRESSING SALMON AND LARGE FISH

Although salmon is the most obvious choice for serving cold, carp, salmon trout and bass are equally well suited to this treatment. Also, it is worth remembering that dressed fish fillets or steaks are an excellent alternative to whole fish. Since the dressing of a whole fish often presents the cook with problems, the following techniques are worth noting.

BONING POACHED SALMON

Follow the recipe for Hot Poached Salmon (page 40). Cool the fish in the court bouillon, following the instructions for serving cold and removing the skin. Using a sharp, pointed knife, cut the flesh around the head down to the bone. Cut the flesh down to the bone around the tail. Make a cut into the flesh along the length of the fish as far as the bone.

Cut horizontally into the flesh, along the backbone of the fish, from head to tail to loosen the top fillet.

Have a piece of foil on the work surface beside the fish ready to hold the fillets. You need a long palette knife or two fish slices to remove the fillet. Carefully slide the knife or slices under the fillet and lift it off in one piece. If the fish is large, cut the fillet in half or into three portions, then remove each piece neatly.

Carefully cut the flesh off the bone over the belly of the fish and lift it off, in one piece or several pieces, as before.

Now remove all the bones. If serving a salmon trout, snip the backbone at the head and tail end. The bones of salmon come away easily in sections.

When all the bones have been removed, carefully replace the fillets in their original position. There will be small gaps and untidy-looking areas but these will be covered by the garnish.

GARNISHING SALMON

The final dressing: cut the finest possible slices of cucumber. Thick slices will not do – they have to be thin enough to curve to the shape of the fish. Dip each slice in lemon juice and lay it on the salmon. Start at the tail, overlapping each row of cucumber to mimic scales.

Pipe mayonnaise stars or shells around the tail and head of the fish, also along the top and base of the body if liked. Small triangles of lemon slices or sliced stuffed olives may be used to cover the eye of the fish. Sprigs of parsley may also be used as a garnish.

CURVED FISH

If the fish has been curved for cooking, it should be garnished with the bones in place.

SCAMPI IN PAPRIKA CREAM

25 g / 1 oz butter
15 ml / 1 tbsp finely chopped onion
5 ml / 1 tsp paprika
100 ml / 3½ fl oz medium-dry sherry
450 g / 1 lb peeled cooked scampi tails
3 egg yolks
200 ml / 7 fl oz double cream
4 small tomatoes, peeled, seeded and cut in quarters
salt and pepper

Melt the butter in a saucepan, add the onion and cook gently for 8–10 minutes, stirring often, until the onion is softened but not browned.

Add the paprika and sherry to the onion and butter. Stir in and boil, uncovered, until reduced by half. Stir in the scampi tails, lower the heat and heat gently for 5 minutes.

Beat the egg yolks and cream in a small bowl. Stir in a little of the hot sauce and mix well. Add the contents of the bowl to the scampi and sauce mixture and heat gently, stirring. Do not allow the sauce to boil. Stir in the tomatoes and heat through gently, then spoon the mixture into a warmed serving dish. Serve at once, with boiled rice or chunks of French bread.

SERVES FOUR

SPICY FISH SLICES

675 g / 1½ lb cod or hake fillets
7.5 ml / 1½ tsp salt
5 ml / 1 tsp turmeric
5 ml / 1 tsp chilli powder
90 ml / 6 tbsp oil
fresh coriander sprigs to garnish

Cut the fish into 2 cm / ¾ inch slices and spread them out in a shallow dish large enough to hold all the slices in a single layer. Mix the salt and spices in a bowl. Stir in enough water to make a thick paste. Rub the paste into the fish, cover and leave to marinate for 1 hour.

Heat the oil in a large frying pan. Add as much of the spiced fish as possible, but do not overfill the pan. Fry the fish for 5–10 minutes until golden brown all over, then remove from the pan with a slotted spoon. Drain on absorbent kitchen paper and keep hot while cooking the rest of the fish.

Garnish and serve hot, with rice or a small salad, if liked.

SERVES FOUR TO FIVE

FRENCH FRIED HADDOCK

1 kg / 2¼ lb haddock fillets, skinned
250 ml / 8 fl oz milk
100 g / 4 oz plain flour
salt and pepper
oil for deep frying
lemon wedges, to serve

Cut the fish into 4–5 portions. Pour the milk into a shallow bowl. Spread out the flour in a second bowl; add salt and pepper. Dip the pieces of fish first into milk and then into flour, shaking off the excess.

Put the oil for frying into a deep wide pan. Heat the oil to 180–190°C / 350–375°F or until a cube of bread added to the oil browns in 30 seconds.

If using a deep-fat fryer, follow the manufacturer's instructions.

Carefully lower the fish into the hot oil and fry for 3–5 minutes until evenly browned. Drain on absorbent kitchen paper and serve on a warmed platter, with lemon wedges.

SERVES FOUR TO FIVE

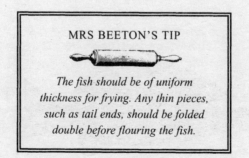

MRS BEETON'S TIP

*The fish should be of uniform
thickness for frying. Any thin pieces,
such as tail ends, should be folded
double before flouring the fish.*

SOLE COLBERT

200 g / 7 oz Maître d'Hôtel butter (page 228)
10 ml / 2 tsp finely chopped fresh tarragon
6 Dover soles
100 g / 4 oz plain flour
salt and pepper
2 eggs, lightly beaten
50 g / 2 oz fresh white breadcrumbs
oil for deep frying

GARNISH
lemon wedges
fresh tarragon sprigs

Mix the maître d'hôtel butter and tarragon. Remove the dark skin of the fish. Cut down the backbone on the skinned side and slice under the flesh, following the bones to make a pocket on each side. Cut the backbone in three places with sharp scissors to allow removal after cooking.

Mix the flour with salt and pepper and spread out in a shallow bowl. Put the beaten eggs in a second shallow bowl and spread out the breadcrumbs on a sheet of foil. Coat each fish in flour, then in egg and breadcrumbs.

Put the oil for frying into a deep wide pan. Heat the oil to 180–190°C / 350–375°F or until a cube of bread added to the oil browns in 30 seconds. If using a deep-fat fryer, follow the manufacturer's instructions. Deep fry the fish, one at a time, until golden brown, reheating the oil as necessary.

Drain the fish on absorbent kitchen paper, remove the bone where cut and arrange on a warmed serving dish. Fill the pockets of the fish with the tarragon-flavoured butter and serve immediately, garnished with lemon and tarragon.

SERVES SIX

FISH CAKES

*Tasty, nutritious, easy to make and popular with children,
home-made fish cakes are perfect for midweek family meals.*

**350 g / 12 oz cooked white fish, flaked
450 g / 1 lb potatoes
25 g / 1 oz butter
30 ml / 2 tbsp single cream or milk
15 ml / 1 tbsp finely chopped parsley
salt and pepper
50 g / 2 oz plain flour
oil for shallow frying**

Remove any bones from the fish. Cook the potatoes in a saucepan of salted boiling water for about 30 minutes or until tender. Drain thoroughly and mash with a potato masher, or beat with a hand-held electric whisk until smooth. Beat in the butter and cream or milk. Add the flaked fish and parsley, with salt and pepper to taste. Set aside until cold.

Form the fish mixture into 8 portions, shaping each to a flat, round cake. Spread out the flour in a shallow bowl, add salt and pepper and use to coat the fish cakes.

Heat the oil in a frying pan, add the fish cakes and fry for 6–8 minutes, turning once. Drain on absorbent kitchen paper, arrange on a warmed serving dish and serve.

SERVES FOUR

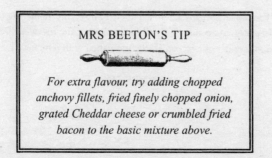

MRS BEETON'S TIP

*For extra flavour, try adding chopped
anchovy fillets, fried finely chopped onion,
grated Cheddar cheese or crumbled fried
bacon to the basic mixture above.*

MARINATED FRIED HERRINGS

Serve as a starter with brown bread and butter.
Soured cream makes a good accompaniment.

8 herrings
30 ml / 2 tbsp plain flour
2.5 ml / ½ tsp salt
2.5 ml / ½ tsp pepper
butter for shallow frying

MARINADE
300 ml / ½ pint cider vinegar
90 g / 3½ oz sugar
1 onion, thinly sliced
1 bay leaf
6 peppercorns

Make the marinade by combining the vinegar and sugar in a saucepan. Add 300 ml / ½ pint water and bring to the boil, stirring until the sugar has dissolved. Set aside to cool.

Split the herrings and remove the backbones. Spread out the flour in a shallow bowl, add salt and pepper, and use to coat the fish lightly all over.

Melt the butter in a large frying pan, add the fish and fry for 7–8 minutes or until golden brown, turning once. Using a slotted spoon and a fish slice, transfer the herrings to a dish large enough to hold them all in a single layer.

Tuck the onion slices, bay leaf and peppercorns around the herrings and pour the cold vinegar mixture over. Cover the dish and set aside in a cool place for about 6 hours. Serve with brown bread and butter, if liked.

SERVES FOUR

MACKEREL WITH GOOSEBERRY SAUCE

*Gooseberry sauce is such a classic accompaniment to mackerel
that in France the fruit is known as groseille à maquereau.*

50 g / 2 oz plain flour
salt and pepper
8 mackerel fillets
50 g / 2 oz butter
juice of 1 lemon
45 ml / 3 tbsp chopped parsley

SAUCE
450 g / 1 lb gooseberries, topped and tailed
45 ml / 3 tbsp dry still cider
25 g / 1 oz butter
15 ml / 1 tbsp caster sugar

Make the sauce by combining the gooseberries, cider and butter in a small
saucepan. Bring the liquid to simmering point and poach the fruit, stirring occasionally, until soft. Purée the mixture by passing it through a sieve set over a
small pan. Stir in the sugar.

Spread out the flour in a shallow bowl, add salt and pepper, and coat the fish
lightly all over.

Melt the butter in a large frying pan, add the fish and fry gently for 5–7 minutes
or until browned, turning once. Using a slotted spoon and a fish slice, transfer
the fish to a warmed serving dish and keep hot.

Heat the gooseberry sauce. Continue to heat the butter in the frying pan until
it becomes light brown. Stir in the lemon juice and parsley and pour over the
fish. Pour the gooseberry sauce into a jug or sauceboat and serve at once, with
the fish.

SERVES FOUR

SOLE MEUNIERE

50 g / 2 oz plain flour
salt and pepper
4 large sole fillets
75 g / 3 oz butter
30 ml / 2 tbsp chopped parsley
juice of 1 lemon
lemon wedges to garnish

Mix the flour with salt and pepper and spread out in a shallow bowl. Lightly coat the fish fillets in the seasoned flour.

Melt the butter in a frying pan and fry the fillets over moderate heat for about 7 minutes, turning once, until golden brown.

Using a slotted spoon and a fish slice, carefully transfer the fish to a warmed serving dish and keep hot. Continue heating the butter until it is nut brown. Add the parsley.

Pour the butter over the fish, sprinkle with lemon juice and serve at once, garnished with lemon wedges.

SERVES FOUR

SABO-NO-TERIYAKI

This dish can also be made with herring, salmon or bream.

150 ml / ¼ pint soy sauce
45 ml / 3 tbsp mirin (see Mrs Beeton's Tip)
pinch of chilli powder
15 ml / 1 tbsp grated fresh root ginger
2 garlic cloves, crushed
4 mackerel fillets

Mix the soy sauce, mirin, chilli powder, ginger and garlic in a bowl. Stir well. Arrange the mackerel fillets in a shallow dish large enough to hold them all in a single layer. Pour the soy sauce mixture over, cover the dish and marinate for 2 hours.

Drain the fish, reserving the marinade. Cook under a hot grill for 5–10 minutes, brushing the fish several times with the reserved marinade during cooking. Serve at once.

SERVES FOUR

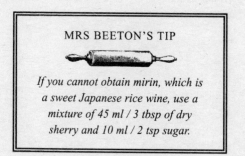

MRS BEETON'S TIP

If you cannot obtain mirin, which is a sweet Japanese rice wine, use a mixture of 45 ml / 3 tbsp of dry sherry and 10 ml / 2 tsp sugar.

TROUT WITH ALMONDS

100 g / 4 oz butter
4 trout, cleaned and trimmed
salt and pepper
juice of 1 lemon
50 g / 2 oz flaked almonds
125 ml / 4 fl oz double cream
3 egg yolks

Melt the butter in a grill pan under moderate heat. Lay the trout in the pan and sprinkle with salt and pepper and lemon juice. Grill for 5 minutes.

Carefully turn the trout over. Sprinkle most of the almonds over the fish, spreading out the rest at the side of the pan. Grill for 3– 5 minutes more until the trout are tender and the almonds browned. Using a fish slice and slotted spoon, transfer the trout and almonds to absorbent kitchen paper to drain. Tip the grill pan juices into a small saucepan. Arrange the trout on a warmed serving platter and keep hot. Set the browned almonds aside.

Add the cream and egg yolks to the pan juices and mix well. Heat gently, stirring constantly until the sauce thickens. Do not let the mixture boil. Spoon the sauce over the trout, garnish with the reserved almonds and serve at once.

SERVES FOUR

SMOKED COD & CORN CASSEROLE

1 (326 g / 1½ oz) can sweetcorn kernels, drained
450 g / 1 lb smoked cod fillet, skinned and cut in 1 cm / ½ inch strips
pepper
25 g / 1 oz butter
125 ml / 4 fl oz single cream

Set the oven at 180°C / 350°F / gas 4. Drain the corn and spread a layer on the base of an ovenproof dish. Add a layer of cod strips. Season with pepper and dot with butter.

Repeat the layers until all the corn and cod have been used, then pour over the cream. Cover and bake for 25 minutes. Serve at once.

SERVES THREE TO FOUR

VARIATION

• **Corn 'n' Cod** Poach the smoked cod fillets, then drain and flake. Make white sauce, using 50 g / 2 oz each of butter and plain flour and 600 ml / 1 pint milk (or milk mixed with the drained liquid from the can of sweetcorn). Add pepper to taste and stir in the cod and corn. Spoon into a dish, top with grated Cheddar cheese and bake for 15–20 minutes at 180°C / 350°F / gas 4.

STUFFED HERRINGS

butter for greasing
4 large herrings

STUFFING
50 g / 2 oz butter
225 g / 8 oz onions, finely chopped
225 g / 8 oz cooking apples
15 ml / 1 tbsp cider or white wine vinegar
salt and pepper

Grease a flat ovenproof dish and a piece of foil large enough to cover it. Set the oven at 190°C / 375°F / gas 5. Scale the herrings, cut off the heads and remove the bones without breaking the skin.

Make the stuffing. Melt the butter in a large frying pan, add the onions and fry gently for about 10 minutes until soft. Peel, core and grate the apples and add them to the pan. Mix well, then add the vinegar, with salt and pepper to taste.

Divide the stuffing between the herrings, filling the cavities and then reshaping the fish. Lay them on the prepared dish, cover loosely with the foil and bake for 25 minutes. Serve at once.

SERVES FOUR

MICROWAVE TIP

Arrange the stuffed herrings in
alternate directions in a suitable dish.
Cover with microwave film and cook
on High for 7–8 minutes.

DUNWICH PLAICE

25 g / 1 oz butter
4 (275 g / 10 oz) plaice, cleaned and trimmed

STUFFING
100 g / 4 oz mild Cheddar cheese, grated
50 g / 2 oz fresh white breadcrumbs
5 ml / 1 tsp mustard powder
salt and pepper
10 ml / 2 tsp shredded fresh basil or 5 ml / 1 tsp dried basil
juice of ½ lemon
30 ml / 2 tbsp beaten egg

GARNISH
2 halved tomatoes
4 rolled anchovies

Use most of the butter to grease a shallow ovenproof baking dish and a piece of foil large enough to cover it. Set the oven at 190°C / 375°F / gas 5. Make a cut down the entire length of each fish as though for filleting. Remove the bone to make a pouch.

Make the stuffing by mixing all the ingredients together in a small bowl. Lift the two loose flaps on one of the fish and fill the pouch with a quarter of the stuffing. Repeat with the remaining fish.

Place the fish in the prepared dish, dot with the remaining butter, cover with the foil and bake for 20–30 minutes. Garnish each portion with half a tomato and a rolled anchovy. Serve at once.

SERVES FOUR

FILLET OF SOLE BONNE FEMME

fat for greasing
16 lemon sole fillets
275 g / 10 oz mushrooms
50 g / 2 oz butter
12 black peppercorns
2–3 parsley stalks
25 g / 1 oz plain flour
300 ml / ½ pint fish stock
salt and pepper
lemon juice
2 shallots, slices
15 ml / 1 tbsp chopped parsley
250 ml / 8 fl oz dry white wine

Grease a shallow ovenproof baking dish and a piece of foil to cover it. Arrange the sole fillets. Set the oven at 180°C / 350°F / gas 4. Slice the mushroom caps (set aside the stems) and scatter them over the fish.

Melt 25 g / 1 oz of the butter in a saucepan, add the mushroom stems, peppercorns and parsley stalks. Cook over gentle heat for 10 minutes. Add the flour and cook over a low heat for 2–3 minutes, without allowing the mixture to colour. Gradually add the stock and simmer, stirring for 3–4 minutes. Sieve into a clean pan. Add salt, pepper and lemon juice to taste.

Sprinkle the shallots and parsley over the fish, sprinkle with salt and pepper and pour in the wine. Cover with the foil and bake for 20 minutes.

Using slotted spoon and fish slice, transfer the fish to a warmed serving dish and keep hot. Boil the cooking liquid in a saucepan until reduced by half.

Meanwhile return the sauce to a gentle heat and bring to simmering point. Stir the sauce into the reduced cooking liquid with the remaining butter. As soon as the butter has melted, pour the sauce over the fish. Place under a hot grill until lightly browned. Serve at once.

SERVES EIGHT

BAKED FRESH SARDINES

fat for greasing
45 ml / 3 tbsp olive oil
2 large onions, finely chopped
45 ml / 3 tbsp medium-dry white wine
225 g / 8 oz tomatoes, peeled, seeded and chopped
salt and pepper
900 g / 2 lb sardines, cleaned and trimmed
50 g / 2 oz fresh white breadcrumbs
25 g / 1 oz butter
watercress sprigs to garnish

Grease a shallow ovenproof baking dish. Set the oven at 180° / 350°F / gas 4.

Heat the oil in a small saucepan, add the onions and fry gently for about 5 minutes until lightly browned. Add the wine and boil until the volume is reduced by two thirds. Stir in the tomatoes, with salt and pepper to taste. Cook for 3–4 minutes.

Pour the tomato mixture into the prepared dish, arrange the sardines on top and sprinkle with the breadcrumbs. Dot with the butter and bake for 25 minutes. Serve hot, garnished with watercress.

SERVES SIX

APRICOT-STUFFED TROUT

*The apricots for the stuffing need to be soaked overnight,
unless you use ready-to-eat dried fruit.*

fat for greasing
6 trout, cleaned and trimmed
2 onions, finely chopped
salt and pepper
250 ml / 8 fl oz dry white wine
75 g / 3 oz butter
25 g / 1 oz plain flour
250 ml / 8 fl oz fish stock
60 ml / 4 tbsp dry white wine
2 egg yolks
juice of ½ lemon
chopped parsley to garnish

STUFFING
75 g / 3 oz dried apricots
75 g / 3 oz fresh white breadcrumbs
pinch of dried thyme
pinch of ground mace
pinch of grated nutmeg
1 celery stick, finely chopped
25 g / 1 oz butter

Make the stuffing. Soak the apricots overnight in a small bowl with water to cover. Next day, drain the fruit, reserving the soaking liquid, and chop finely. Mix the apricots in a bowl with the breadcrumbs, salt, pepper, herbs, spices and celery. Melt the butter in a small saucepan and stir it into the mixture. Moisten further with a little of the reserved soaking liquid (see Mrs Beeton's Tip).

Grease a shallow ovenproof baking dish. Set the oven at 180°C / 350°F / gas 4. Fill the trout with the apricot stuffing. Spread out the onions on the base of the prepared dish, arrange the trout on top and sprinkle with plenty of salt and pepper. Pour the wine into the dish, dot the fish with 25 g / 1 oz of the butter, cover and oven poach for 25 minutes.

MRS BEETON'S TIP

*If you use ready-to-eat dried apricots,
moisten the stuffing with a little
chicken stock.*

Meanwhile, melt 25 g / 1 oz of the remaining butter in a pan. Stir in the flour and cook over low heat for 2–3 minutes, without allowing the mixture to colour. Gradually add the fish stock, stirring constantly until the sauce boils and thickens. Add salt and pepper to taste. Reduce the heat, add let the wine and the sauce simmer for 10 minutes.

Bring the sauce to just below boiling point and whisk in the remaining butter, a little at a time. Remove the pan from the heat. Blend the egg yolks and lemon juice in a small bowl, add a little of the hot sauce and mix well. Add the contents of the bowl to the sauce and mix well. Cover with damp greaseproof paper and set aside.

Using a slotted spoon and fish slice, carefully transfer the fish to a wooden board. Strain the cooking liquid into a pan. Skin the trout, then arrange them on a warmed flameproof serving dish and keep hot.

Boil the cooking liquid until it is reduced by a quarter, then add it to the white wine sauce. Place over moderate heat and warm through, stirring the sauce until it thickens. Do not allow it to boil. Pour the hot sauce over the fish. Place under a moderate grill for 4–5 minutes to brown lightly. Garnish with chopped parsley and serve at once.

SERVES SIX

STARGAZEY PIE

This is a traditional Cornish recipe. It is not a recipe for anyone who is deterred by fish bones but it tastes delicious. The top crust is traditionally glazed with thick Cornish cream, but single cream or top-of-the milk may be used instead.

5 even-sized pilchards or herrings, scaled and cleaned
1 onion, finely chopped
1 small sharp cooking apple
90 ml / 6 tbsp fresh white breadcrumbs
salt and pepper
150–175 ml / 5–6 fl oz dry still cider
2 hard-boiled eggs
2 rindless back bacon rashers, finely chopped
10 ml / 2 tsp cider vinegar
6 parsley sprigs to garnish

SHORT CRUST PASTRY
150 g / 5 oz plain flour
1.25 ml / ¼ tsp salt
65 g / 2½ oz margarine
plain flour for rolling out
cream for glazing

Make the pastry. Sift the flour and salt into a bowl, then rub in the margarine until the mixture resembles fine breadcrumbs. Add enough cold water to make a stiff dough. Press the dough together with your fingertips, wrap in a polythene bag and chill.

Rinse in cold water a pie dish or ovenproof plate that will just hold two fish placed end to end across the centre, with their tails overlapping in the centre and their heads sticking over the edge. Turn the pie dish upside down to drain until required.

Set the oven at 160°C / 325°F / gas 3. Split the fish, without removing the heads or tails, and ease out the backbones. Set 30 ml / 2 tbsp of the chopped onion aside and put the rest in a bowl. Peel and grate the apple and add it to the bowl with the breadcrumbs. Add salt and pepper to taste and moisten the stuffing with 45–60 ml / 3–4 tbsp of the cider. Stuff the fish with the mixture and reshape neatly. Reserve any leftover stuffing.

Roll out the pastry on a lightly floured surface and use just over half of it to line the chosen dish. Arrange the fish in a star shape with heads right on the edge of the dish and tails overlapping in the centre. Lift the tails and form them into an upright cluster, securing them with wooden cocktail sticks if necessary. Twist a piece of foil over and around them.

Fill the triangular spaces between the fish with egg, bacon, the reserved onion and any leftover stuffing. Sprinkle with the vinegar and pour the remaining cider into the dish.

Roll out the remaining pastry on a floured surface and make a crust for the pie. Make a hole in the centre of the crust large enough to fit around the fish tails. Dampen the edges of the pastry.

Very carefully lift the pastry on the rolling pin and lay it on the pie, with the fish tails sticking through the middle. Press the pastry crust between the fish heads, pushing it back slightly around the heads so that they stick out. Brush the top crust with cream and bake for 1 hour. Garnish with sprigs of parsley around the tails and serve very hot.

SERVES SIX

Poultry

*Poultry is ideal for all occasions,
for everyday light dishes or celebration
meals. This chapter features recipes from
homely favourites to exotic new ideas.*

ROAST CHICKEN WITH HONEY AND ALMONDS

1 (1.5–1.8 kg / 3½–4 lb) oven-ready roasting chicken
½ lemon
salt and pepper
45 ml / 3 tbsp honey
50 g / 2 oz flaked almonds
pinch of powdered saffron
30 ml / 2 tbsp oil
watercress sprigs to garnish (optional)

Set the oven at 180°C / 350°F / gas 4. Rub the chicken all over with the cut lemon, then sprinkle with salt and pepper. Line a roasting tin with a piece of foil large enough to enclose the bird completely.

Put the bird into the foil-lined tin, then brush it all over with the honey. Sprinkle the nuts and saffron over, then trickle the oil very gently over the top. Bring up the foil carefully, tenting it over the bird so that it is completely covered. Make sure that the foil does not touch the skin. Seal the package by folding the edges of the foil over.

Roast for 1½–2 hours or until the chicken is cooked through. Open the foil for the last 10 minutes to allow the breast of the bird to brown. Transfer the chicken to a heated serving dish and garnish it with watercress if liked.

SERVES FOUR TO SIX

CHICKEN CHASSEUR

butter for greasing
1 (1.6 kg / 3½ lb) roasting chicken
25 g / 1 oz plain flour
salt and pepper
50 g / 2 oz butter
15 ml / 1 tbsp oil
1 small onion, finely chopped
175 g / 6 oz button mushrooms, sliced
150 ml / ¼ pint dry white wine
15 ml / 1 tbsp tomato purée
275 ml / 9 fl oz chicken stock
1 sprig each of fresh tarragon, chervil and parsley, chopped

Divide the chicken into 8 serving portions. Mix the flour, salt and pepper in a sturdy polythene bag. Add the chicken portions and toss until well coated. Shake off excess flour.

Melt the butter in the oil in a large frying pan. When hot, add the chicken pieces and fry until browned all over and cooked through. Using a slotted spoon, remove the chicken pieces from the pan, drain on absorbent kitchen paper and transfer to a warmed serving dish. Cover and keep hot.

Add the onion to the fat remaining in the pan and fry gently until soft but not coloured. Add the mushrooms and fry briefly. Pour in the wine and add the tomato purée and stock. Stir until well blended, then simmer gently for 10 minutes. Stir in two-thirds of the chopped herbs, with salt and pepper to taste.

Pour the sauce over the chicken portions and sprinkle with the remaining herbs. Serve hot.

SERVES FOUR

BARBECUED CHICKEN DRUMSTICKS

75 g / 3 oz butter
12 chicken drumsticks
60 ml / 4 tbsp vinegar
15 ml / 1 tbsp Worcestershire sauce
15 ml / 1 tbsp tomato purée
5 ml / 1 tsp soy sauce
5 ml / 1 tsp grated onion
5 ml / 1 tsp paprika
2.5 ml / ½ tsp salt

Melt the butter in a small saucepan. Brush a little of it over the chicken drumsticks to coat them thoroughly, then arrange on a rack in a grill pan.

Stir the remaining ingredients into the leftover butter in the pan. Simmer for 2 minutes, then brush a little of the mixture over the chicken. Grill or barbecue over medium coals, turning occasionally and brushing with more sauce until cooked through. Serve with rice or salad.

SERVES FOUR

CHICKEN KIEV

*The original chicken Kiev was a boned and flattened chicken breast
with a simple herb – usually chive – butter filling. Today the butter
is frequently flavoured with garlic, as in the version below.*

**4 chicken breast and wing joints
salt and pepper
plain flour for coating
1 egg, beaten
about 75 g / 3 oz dried white breadcrumbs
oil for deep frying**

BUTTER FILLING
**100 g / 4 oz butter, softened
finely grated rind of ½ lemon
15 ml / 1 tbsp chopped parsley
2 small garlic cloves, crushed**

GARNISH
**lemon wedges
parsley sprigs**

Make the butter filling. Beat the butter lightly in a bowl. Gradually work in the
lemon rind, parsley and garlic, with salt and pepper to taste. Form the butter
into a roll, wrap it in greaseproof paper and chill well.

To prepare the chicken, cut off the wing ends and remove the skin from the
breast meat. Turn the joints flesh side up and cut out all bones except the wing
bone, which is left in place. Do not cut right through the flesh. To flatten the
boned meat slightly, place it between greaseproof paper and beat lightly with a
cutlet bat or rolling pin.

Cut the flavoured butter into four long pieces and place one on each piece of
chicken. Fold the flesh over the butter to enclose it completely and secure with
wooden cocktail sticks. The wing bone should protrude at one end of each
chicken cutlet.

Spread out the flour in a shallow bowl and add salt and pepper. Put the beaten egg in a second bowl and stir in a little water. Place the breadcrumbs on a sheet of foil. Coat the chicken in flour, then in egg and breadcrumbs. Repeat the coating at least once more, using more egg and breadcrumbs, so that the chicken and butter filling are well sealed. Chill lightly.

Heat the oil to 160°C / 325°F or until a cube of bread added to the oil browns in 2 minutes. Deep fry the chicken, turning or basting the cutlets until golden brown and firm to the touch, as necessary for even cooking. Allow 15–20 minutes to ensure the flesh is cooked through. Drain thoroughly and keep hot, if necessary, while frying any remaining cutlets. To serve, place the cutlets on a heated serving dish. Remove the cocktail sticks and garnish with lemon wedges and parsley.

SERVES FOUR

VARIATIONS

- **Alternative Fillings** Instead of using butter, flavoured soft cheese makes a deliciously creamy filling. For example, try bought soft cheese with herbs and garlic or mix some chopped fresh herbs with plain cream or curd cheese. Finely chopped ham or crumbled crisply grilled bacon also makes an excellent filling when combined with soft cheese.
- **Baked Kiev** The coated chicken may be baked instead of being deep fried. It is essential to make the breadcrumb coating even and fairly thick. Place the portions in a well-greased roasting tin and dot with a little butter or trickle a little oil over the top. Bake at 190°C / 375°F / gas 5 for 45–50 minutes, until the coating is well browned and crisp. The chicken must be fully cooked – pierce one portion towards one end near the bone to check.

LEMON CHICKEN

6 chicken breasts
salt and pepper
50 g / 2 oz butter
15 ml / 1 tbsp oil
1 onion, sliced
1 lemon, sliced
60 ml / 4 tbsp plain flour
250 ml / 8 fl oz chicken stock
2–3 bay leaves
5 ml / 1 tsp caster sugar

Set the oven at 190°C / 375°F / gas 5. Season the chicken breasts with salt and pepper. Melt the butter in the oil in a large frying pan, add the chicken and fry until golden brown all over. Using tongs or a slotted spoon, transfer to a casserole.

Add the onion and lemon slices to the fat remaining in the pan and fry over very gentle heat for about 15 minutes. Using a slotted spoon, transfer the onion and lemon to the casserole.

Sprinkle the flour into the fat remaining in the pan. Cook for 1 minute, then blend in the stock. Bring to the boil, stirring all the time. Add the bay leaves and sugar, with salt and pepper to taste. Pour over the chicken breasts in the casserole, cover and bake for about 45 minutes or until the chicken is tender. Remove the casserole lid 5 minutes before the end of the cooking time.

Remove the bay leaves before serving or reserve them as a garnish.

SERVES SIX

TANDOORI CHICKEN

1 (1.4–1.6 kg / 3–3½ lb) chicken
15 ml / 1 tbsp cumin seeds
30 ml / 2 tbsp grated fresh root ginger
1 onion, grated
4 garlic cloves, crushed
5 ml / 1 tsp salt
5 ml / 1 tsp chilli powder
2.5 ml / 1 tsp turmeric
5 ml / 1 tsp garam masala
few drops of red food colouring (optional)
juice of 2 lemons
150 ml / ¼ pint plain yogurt
30 ml / 2 tbsp oil

Skin the chicken. Keep it whole or cut it into 4 or 8 pieces. Toast the cumin seeds in a small ungreased frying pan over moderate heat for 1 minute. Grind them in a pepper mill, or use a pestle and mortar. Set the seeds aside.

Combine the ginger, onion, garlic, salt, chilli powder, turmeric and garam masala in a small bowl. Add the colouring, if used, then stir in the lemon juice and yogurt.

Prick the chicken with a fork and cut a few slits in the legs and breast. Rub the bird with the paste, pressing it deeply into the slits. Place in a shallow dish, cover tightly with foil and a lid and marinate for 12 hours or overnight.

Set the oven at 180ºC / 350ºF / gas 4. Put the chicken on a rack in a shallow roasting tin. Baste it with the oil and any remaining paste. Bake for 1½–2 hours, spooning over the oil and pan juices from time to time. When cooked, sprinkle with the toasted cumin seeds. Serve with rice and a tomato and onion salad.

SERVES FOUR

COQ AU VIN

*The best coq au vin is made by marinating the
chicken overnight in the red wine before cooking.*

1 (1.6 kg / 3½ lb) chicken with giblets
1 bouquet garni
salt and pepper
75 g / 3 oz unsalted butter
15 ml / 1 tbsp oil
150 g / 5 oz belly of pickled pork or green (unsmoked) bacon rashers,
rind removed and chopped
150 g / 5 oz button onions or shallots
30 ml / 2 tbsp brandy
175 g / 6 oz small button mushrooms
2 garlic cloves, crushed
575 ml / 19 fl oz burgundy or other red wine
15 ml / 1 tbsp tomato purée
25 g / 1 oz plain flour
croûtes of fried bread (like croûtons, page 28, but larger), to serve

Joint the chicken and skin the portions if liked. Place the giblets in a saucepan
with 450 ml / ¾ pint water. Add the bouquet garni, salt and pepper. Cook gently
for about 1 hour, then strain. Measure the stock and set aside 275 ml / 9 fl oz.

Set the oven at 150°C / 300°F / gas 2. Melt 40 g / 1½ oz of the butter in the oil
in a flameproof casserole. Add the pork or bacon, with the onions. Cook over
gentle heat for about 10 minutes until the onions are lightly coloured. Using a
slotted spoon, transfer the bacon and onions to a plate.

Add the chicken portions to the fat remaining in the pan and brown lightly all
over. Ignite the brandy (see Mrs Beeton's Tip). When the flames die down, pour
it into the casserole. Add the reserved bacon and onions, with the mushrooms
and garlic. Stir in the wine, giblet stock and tomato purée. Cover and cook in
the oven for 1–1½ hours or until the chicken is cooked through and tender.

Using a slotted spoon, transfer the chicken portions to a heated serving dish.
Arrange the bacon, mushrooms and onions over them. Cover with buttered

---

MRS BEETON'S TIP

*To flame the brandy, either pour it into a soup
ladle and warm over low heat or warm it in a
jug in the microwave for 15 seconds on High.
Ignite the brandy (if warmed in a soup ladle it
may well ignite spontaneously) and when the
flames die down, pour it into the casserole.*

---

greaseproof paper and keep hot. Return the casserole to the hob and simmer the
liquid until reduced by about one-third.

Meanwhile make a beurre manié by blending the remaining butter with the flour
in a small bowl. Gradually add small pieces of the mixture to the stock, whisking thoroughly after each addition. Continue to whisk the sauce until it thickens.
Pour it over the chicken. Garnish with croûtes of fried bread and serve.

SERVES FOUR TO SIX

ENGLISH ROAST DUCK

fat for basting
Sage and Onion Stuffing (page 229)
1 (1.8 kg / 4 lb) oven-ready duck
salt and pepper
30 ml / 2 tbsp plain flour
300 ml / ½ pint duck or chicken stock (see Mrs Beeton's Tip)

Set the oven at 190°C / 375°F / gas 5. Spoon the stuffing into the duck and truss it. Weigh the duck and calculate the cooking time at 20 minutes per 450 g / 1 lb. Sprinkle the breast with salt. Put the duck on a wire rack in a roasting tin and prick the skin all over with a fork or skewer to release the fat. Roast for the required time, basting the duck occasionally with the pan juices and pouring away the excess fat as necessary. Test by piercing the thickest part of the thigh with the point of a sharp knife. The juices should run clear.

Transfer the duck to a heated platter, remove the trussing string and keep hot. Pour off most of the fat from the roasting tin, sprinkle in the flour and cook, stirring, for 2 minutes. Blend in the stock. Bring to the boil, then lower the heat and simmer, stirring, for 3–4 minutes. Add salt and pepper to taste. Serve in a gravy-boat, with the duck.

SERVES FOUR

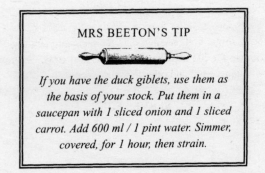

MRS BEETON'S TIP

If you have the duck giblets, use them as the basis of your stock. Put them in a saucepan with 1 sliced onion and 1 sliced carrot. Add 600 ml / 1 pint water. Simmer, covered, for 1 hour, then strain.

FRENCH CUTLETS

50 g / 2 oz dried white breadcrumbs
grated rind of ½ lemon
salt and pepper
pinch of cayenne pepper
1.25 ml / ¼ tsp ground mace
1 egg yolk
4 boneless chicken breasts, skinned
30 ml / 2 tbsp oil
50 g / 2 oz butter
2 shallots or ½ small onion, chopped
1 small carrot, diced
30 ml / 2 tbsp plain flour
300 ml / ½ pint chicken stock
1 bouquet garni
100 g / 4 oz mushrooms, diced
4 fried bread croûtes (like croûtons, page 28, but larger),
to serve (optional)

Mix the breadcrumbs, lemon rind, salt, cayenne pepper and mace on a plate. Brush the egg yolk over the chicken portions, then coat them in the breadcrumb mixture. Heat the oil and half the butter in a frying pan and fry the chicken for about 15 minutes on each side, until golden and cooked through.

Meanwhile, heat the remaining butter in a small saucepan. Add the shallots or onion and carrot, then cook for 5 minutes. Stir in the flour, gradually stir in the stock and bring to the boil, stirring. Add the bouquet garni and mushrooms, cover and simmer for 20 minutes. Serve the chicken on bread croûtes, if used. Remove the bouquet garni and offer the sauce separately.

SERVES FOUR

FILLETS OF DUCK WITH RICH CHERRY DRESSING

Creamy mashed potatoes or plain cooked noodles and crisp, lightly cooked green beans are suitable accompaniments for this simple, yet rich, dish.

4 boneless duck breasts
salt and pepper
2.5 ml / ½ tsp ground mace
4 bay leaves
4 fresh thyme sprigs
125 ml / 4 fl oz red wine
60 ml / 4 tbsp port
25 g / 1 oz butter
15 ml / 1 tbsp finely chopped onion
225 g / 8 oz cherries, stoned
5 ml / 1 tsp grated lemon rind
10 ml / 2 tsp arrowroot

Prick the skin on the duck breasts all over, or remove it, if preferred. Rub plenty of salt, pepper and mace into the breasts, then place them in a shallow dish, skin uppermost, with a bay leaf and thyme sprig under each. Pour the wine and port over the duck, cover and allow to marinate for at least 2 hours; it may be chilled overnight.

Melt the butter in a frying pan and add the onion with the herbs from the duck. Cook over low heat for 5 minutes. Meanwhile, drain the duck breasts, reserving the marinade. Place them skin down in the pan and increase the heat to moderate. Cook until the skin is well browned, then turn the breasts and cook the second side. Allow about 15 minutes on each side to cook the duck breasts.

Using a slotted spoon, transfer the cooked duck to a heated serving dish or individual plates. Keep hot. Leaving the herbs in the pan, add the cherries and lemon rind. Toss the cherries in the cooking juices for about a minute, until the heat causes them to begin to change colour.

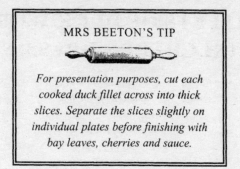

MRS BEETON'S TIP

*For presentation purposes, cut each
cooked duck fillet across into thick
slices. Separate the slices slightly on
individual plates before finishing with
bay leaves, cherries and sauce.*

Pour in the reserved marinade and heat gently until just boiling. While the sauce is heating, put the arrowroot in a cup and blend to a paste with 15–30 ml / 1–2 tbsp cold water. Add it to the pan, stirring. Bring to the boil and remove the pan from the heat.

Discard the thyme sprigs but arrange the bay leaves on the duck. Use a slotted spoon to divide the cherries between the duck breasts, then pour the sauce over and serve at once.

SERVES FOUR

VARIATION

- **Fillets of Duck Bigarade** Cut the pared rind from 1 Seville orange into fine strips and simmer these in water until tender; drain and set aside. Marinate the duck as above, adding the juice of the orange but omitting the port. Continue as above, stirring 30 ml / 2 tbsp plain flour into the cooking juices from the duck, then add 250 ml / 8 fl oz duck or chicken stock and 5 ml / 1 tsp tomato purée. Bring to the boil, stirring, then add the reserved marinade. Lower the heat and simmer rapidly for 10 minutes. Stir in the juice of ½ lemon and 5 ml / 1 tsp redcurrant jelly. Taste for seasoning and pour over the duck.

DUCK WITH ORANGE SAUCE

1 (1.6–1.8 kg / 3½–4 lb) oven-ready duck
salt and pepper
5 oranges
15 ml / 1 tbsp caster sugar
15 ml / 1 tbsp white wine vinegar
30 ml / 2 tbsp brandy
15 ml / 1 tbsp plain flour

Set the oven at 190°C / 375°F / gas 5. Weigh the duck and calculate the cooking time at 20 minutes per 450 g / 1 lb. Sprinkle the breast with salt. Put the duck on a wire rack in a roasting tin and prick the skin all over with a fork or skewer to release the fat. Roast for the required time, basting the duck occasionally with the pan juices and pouring away the excess fat as necessary.

Meanwhile, thinly peel the rind from one of the oranges, taking care not to include any of the bitter pith. Cut the rind into strips, then cook these in boiling water for 1 minute. Drain and set aside on absorbent kitchen paper. Slice one of the remaining oranges and set the slices aside for the garnish. Squeeze the rest of the oranges, including the one with the rind removed, and set the juice aside.

Put the sugar in a saucepan with the vinegar. Heat gently, stirring until the sugar has dissolved, then bring to the boil and boil rapidly without stirring until the syrup turns a golden caramel colour. Remove from the heat and carefully add the orange juice and brandy. Return to the heat and stir until just blended, then add the blanched orange rind strips.

When the duck is cooked, transfer it to a platter, remove the trussing string and cut it into serving portions. Transfer to a heated serving dish and keep hot. Pour off the fat from the roasting tin, sprinkle in the flour and cook, stirring, for 2 minutes. Blend in the orange mixture. Bring to the boil, then lower the heat and simmer, stirring, for 3–4 minutes. Add the salt and pepper to taste. Spoon the sauce over the duck, garnish with the reserved orange slices and serve.

SERVES FOUR

POULTRY PILAU

350 g / 12 oz basmati rice
50 g / 2 oz butter
4 boneless poultry breast fillets, skinned
6 cardamoms
4 cloves
15 ml / 1 tbsp coriander seeds, crushed
15 ml / 1 tbsp allspice berries, crushed
1 cinnamon stick
1 blade of mace
salt and pepper
1.1 litres / 2 pints chicken stock
15 ml / 1 tbsp oil
4 onions, thinly sliced
8 thin rindless bacon rashers
2 eggs, hard-boiled and quartered

Wash the basmati rice in several changes of water, then drain it in a sieve. Melt half the butter in a flameproof casserole or heavy-bottomed saucepan. Add the poultry breasts and brown them well all over. Sprinkle all the spices, salt and pepper around the poultry and cook for 2 minutes, then add the rice. Pour in the stock and bring to the boil. Reduce the heat, cover the pan tightly and cook the pilau gently for about 30 minutes, until the chicken is cooked and the stock is absorbed. Leave to stand, covered, off the heat for 5 minutes before removing the lid.

Meanwhile, melt the remaining butter with the oil in a large frying pan. Add the onions and a little salt and pepper. Then cook, turning the slices occasionally, until golden brown. Roll the bacon rashers and thread them on metal skewers. Cook under a hot grill until crisp and golden, then drain on absorbent kitchen paper.

Mound the cooked pilau on a heated serving dish. Top with the browned onions. Garnish with the bacon rolls and eggs.

SERVES FOUR

Meat

From traditional roast beef with Yorkshire pudding to rich, tangy moussaka, and from juicy steaks to fragrant, herbed shoulder of lamb, these mouthwatering recipes produce excellent results.

STEAKS WITH MUSTARD SAUCE

4 (150–175 g / 5–6 oz) fillet or sirloin steaks, trimmed freshly-ground
black pepper
25 g / 1 oz unsalted butter
30 ml / 2 tbsp oil
150 ml / ¼ tsp pint soured cream
5 ml / 1 tsp lemon juice
10 ml / 2 tsp French mustard
salt
watercress to garnish

Beat each steak lightly on both sides with a cutlet bat or rolling pin. Season with pepper (see Mrs Beeton's Tip). Melt the butter in the oil in a heavy-bottomed frying pan. When hot, add the steaks to the pan and fry quickly on both sides, allowing 2–3 minutes a side for rare steak, 3½–4 minutes for medium-rare and 5–6 minutes a side for well done.

Lift out the steaks, transfer them to a warmed serving dish and keep hot. Stir the soured cream into the juices remaining in the pan and heat through gently, without boiling. Stir in the lemon juice, mustard and salt to taste.

Pour the mustard sauce over the steak, garnish with watercress and serve at once.

SERVES FOUR

MRS BEETON'S TIP

*Do not salt the steaks before frying
as this draws out the juices.*

ROAST RIBS OF BEEF WITH YORKSHIRE PUDDING

*This impressive joint is also known as a standing rib roast.
Ask the butcher to trim the thin ends of the bones so that the joint will
stand upright. The recipe below, as in Mrs Beeton's day, uses clarified
dripping for cooking, but the roast may be cooked without any additional
fat, if preferred. There will be sufficient fat from the meat for basting.*

2.5 kg / 5½ lb forerib of beef
50–75 g / 2–3 oz beef dripping
salt and pepper
vegetable stock or water (see method)

YORKSHIRE PUDDING
100 g / 4 oz plain flour
1 egg, beaten
150 ml / ¼ pint milk

Set the oven at 230ºC / 450ºF / gas 8. Wipe the meat but do not salt it. Melt
50 g / 2 oz of the dripping in a roasting tin, add the meat and quickly spoon
some of the hot fat over it. Roast for 10 minutes.

Lower the oven temperature to 180ºC / 350ºF / gas 4. Baste the meat thoroughly, then continue to roast for a further 1¾ hours for rare meat; 2¼ hours for
well-done meat. Baste frequently during cooking.

Meanwhile make the Yorkshire pudding batter. Sift the flour into a bowl and
add a pinch of salt. Make a well in the centre of the flour and add the beaten
egg. Stir in the milk, gradually working in the flour. Beat vigorously until the
mixture is smooth and bubbly, then stir in 150 ml / ¼ pint water.

About 30 minutes before the end of the cooking time, spoon off 30 ml / 2 tbsp
of the dripping and divide it between six 7.5 cm / 3 inch Yorkshire pudding tins.
Place the tins in the oven for 5 minutes or until the fat is very hot, then carefully divide the batter between them. Bake above the meat for 15–20 minutes.

MRS BEETON'S TIP

*Yorkshire pudding is traditionally cooked in a large tin
below the joint, so that some of the cooking juices
from the meat fall into the pudding to give it an
excellent flavour. In a modern oven, this means using
a rotisserie or resting the meat directly on the oven
shelf. The pudding should be cooked in a large
roasting tin, then cut into portions and served as a
course on its own before the meat course. Gravy
should be poured over the portions of pudding.*

When the beef is cooked, salt it lightly, transfer it to a warmed serving platter
and keep hot. Pour off almost all the water in the roasting tin, leaving the sediment. Pour in enough vegetable stock or water to make a thin gravy, then heat
to boiling point, stirring all the time. Season with salt and pepper and serve in
a heated gravy-boat with the roast and Yorkshire puddings.

SERVES SIX TO EIGHT

BEEF WELLINGTON

*This classic Beef Wellington differs from beef en croûte in that the meat is
covered with fine pâté – preferably pâté de foie gras – before it is wrapped.*

800 g–1 kg / 1¾ lb–2¼ lb fillet of beef
freshly-ground pepper
25 g / 1 oz butter
15 ml / 1 tbsp oil
100 g / 4 oz button mushrooms, sliced
5 ml / 1 tsp chopped fresh mixed herbs
5ml / 1 tsp chopped parsley
75 g / 3 oz fine liver pâté

PUFF PASTRY
225 g / 8 oz plain flour
2.5 ml / ½ tsp salt
225 g / 8 oz butter
3.75 ml / ¾ tsp lemon juice
beaten egg for glazing

Make the pastry. Sift the flour and salt into a mixing bowl and rub in 50 g /
2 oz of the butter. Add the lemon juice and mix to a smooth dough with cold
water. Shape the remaining butter into a rectangle on greaseproof paper. Roll
out the dough on a lightly floured surface to a strip a little wider than the butter
and rather more than twice its length. Place the butter on one half of the pastry,
fold the other half over it, and press the edges together with the rolling pin.
Leave in a cool place for 15 minutes to allow the butter to harden.

Roll out the pastry into a long strip. Fold the bottom third up and the top third
down, press the edges together with the rolling pin and turn the pastry so that
the folded edges are on the right and left. Roll and fold again, cover and leave
in a cool place for 15 minutes. Repeat this process until the pastry has been
rolled out six times. Chill the pastry well between each rolling, wrapping it in
cling film to prevent it drying on the surface. After the final rolling, leave
wrapped pastry in the refrigerator until required.

Set the oven at 230°C / 450°F / gas 8. Wipe, trim and tie the meat into a neat shape. Season with pepper. Melt the butter in the oil in a large frying pan, add the fillet and brown it quickly all over. Carefully transfer the fillet to a roasting tin, reserving the fat in the pan, and roast it for 10–20 minutes (for a rare to medium result). Remove and cool. Leave the oven on.

Heat the fat remaining in the frying pan, add the mushrooms and fry over moderate heat for 2–3 minutes. Remove from the heat, add the herbs and leave to cool.

Roll out the pastry on a lightly floured surface to a rectangle large enough to enclose the fillet. Using a slotted spoon, transfer the mushroom mixture to one half of the pastry. Lay the beef on top and spread the pâté over the meat. Wrap the pastry around the beef to form a neat parcel, sealing the edges well. Place on a baking sheet with the join underneath. Top with leaves and/or a lattice of strips cut from the pastry trimmings, glaze with beaten egg and bake for about 30 minutes. Serve hot or cold.

SERVES SIX

VARIATION

- To make individual beef wellingtons, use six portions of raw fillet. Wrap individually, including mushrooms and pâté, bringing up the pastry sides to make neat parcels. Glaze and bake, allowing 15–20 minutes for rare beef; 25–30 minutes for medium-cooked beef.

STEAK AU POIVRE

20 ml / 4 tsp whole black and white peppercorns, mixed
4 (150–200 g / 5–7 oz) steaks (fillet, sirloin or entrecôte), wiped and
trimmed
1 garlic clove, cut in half
60 ml / 4 tbsp olive oil
50 g / 2 oz butter

PARSLEY BUTTER
50 g / 2 oz butter, softened
30 ml / 2 tbsp chopped parsley
salt and pepper

Make the parsley butter. Beat the butter until creamy in a small bowl. Add the parsley, beating until well combined, then season the mixture with salt and a small pinch of pepper. Form into a roll, wrap in greaseproof paper, and refrigerate until required.

Crush the peppercorns in a mortar with a pestle. Set aside. Rub the steaks on both sides with the cut clove of garlic, then brush both sides generously with olive oil. With the heel of your hand, press the crushed peppercorns into the surface of the meat on each side.

Melt the butter with any remaining olive oil in a heavy-bottomed frying pan. When hot, add the steaks to the pan and fry quickly on both sides, allowing 2–3 minutes a side for rare steak; 3½–4 minutes for medium-rare and 5–6 minutes a side for well done.

Using a palette knife or two spoons, transfer the steaks to a warmed serving dish. Slice the parsley butter into rounds and place one on top of each steak. Serve at once.

SERVES FOUR

BEEF STROGANOFF

675 g / 1½ lb thinly sliced rump steak, trimmed
45 ml / 3 tbsp plain flour
salt and pepper
50 g / 2 oz butter
225 g / 8 oz onions, thinly sliced
225 g / 8 oz mushrooms, thinly sliced
250 ml / 8 fl oz soured cream

Beat the steak slices with a cutlet bat or rolling pin, then cut them into thin strips. Put the flour in a shallow bowl, season with plenty of salt and pepper and coat the beef strips.

Melt half the butter in a large heavy-bottomed saucepan, add the onion slices and fry for about 10 minutes until golden. Stir in the mushrooms and continue cooking for a further 2–3 minutes. Using a slotted spoon, transfer the vegetables to a dish. Set aside.

Melt the remaining butter in the pan, add the meat and fry rapidly for 2–3 minutes, turning frequently. Return the vegetables to the pan and heat through for 1 minute. Pour in the soured cream, stir once or twice, and heat for 1–2 minutes until all the ingredients are heated through (see Mrs Beeton's Tip). Serve at once, with noodles, boiled new potatoes or rice.

SERVES FOUR

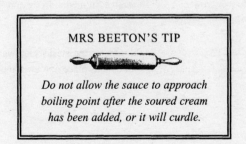

MRS BEETON'S TIP

Do not allow the sauce to approach boiling point after the soured cream has been added, or it will curdle.

GOULASH

*It is the paprika that gives this hearty Hungarian stew
its delicious flavour. Serve simply, with crusty bread.*

50 g / 2 oz dripping or lard
675 g / 1½ lb chuck or blade steak, trimmed
and cut into 2 cm / ¾ inch cubes
2 onions, sliced
30 ml / 2 tbsp plain flour
125 ml / 4 fl oz beef stock
125 ml / 4 fl oz red wine
450 g / 1 lb tomatoes, peeled and diced
or 1 (397 g / 14 oz) can chopped tomatoes
2.5 ml / ½ tsp salt
15 ml / 1 tbsp paprika
1 bouquet garni
450 g / 1 lb potatoes
150 ml / ¼ pint soured cream

Heat the dripping in a flameproof casserole and fry the meat until browned on
all sides. Using a slotted spoon, remove the meat and set aside. Add the onions
to the fat remaining in the casserole and fry gently until just beginning to
brown. Add the flour and cook, stirring until browned. Gradually add the stock
and wine, with the tomatoes, salt, paprika and bouquet garni. Bring to the boil,
stirring, then lower the heat and simmer for 1½–2 hours or until the meat is
tender. Alternatively, transfer the goulash to a casserole and bake at 160°C /
325°F / gas 3 for 1½–2 hours.

Thirty minutes before the end of the cooking time, peel the potatoes, cut them
into cubes and add them to the goulash. When cooked they should be tender
but not broken. Just before serving, remove the bouquet garni and stir in the
soured cream.

SERVES SIX

HAMBURGERS

If you intend serving the burgers less than well cooked,
buy best-quality steak mince.

450 g / 1 lb minced steak
2.5 ml / ½ tsp salt
2.5 ml / ½ tsp freshly-ground black pepper
5–10 ml / 1–2 tsp grated onion (optional)

Combine the meat, salt and pepper in a bowl. Add the onion, if used, and mix well. Shape the mixture lightly into four flat round cakes, about 2 cm / ¾ inch thick.

Heat a frying pan or griddle until very hot, add the hamburgers and cook for 2 minutes on each side for rare meat; 4 minutes per side for well done meat. Alternatively, cook under a preheated grill or over coals on a barbecue grill for 6–8 minutes, turning once. Serve plain or in buns, with toppings or fillings as desired.

SERVES FOUR

VARIATIONS

- Offer any or all of the following: lettuce leaves; sliced cucumber; sliced tomatoes; sliced gherkins; sliced raw or fried onions; hamburger relish; German or French mustard; tomato ketchup; mayonnaise; soured cream.
- **Lamb Burgers** Use good quality minced lamb instead of steak. Add 2.5 ml / ½ tsp dried oregano to the mixture.
- **Cheese Burgers** Top each hamburger with a slice of processed cheese during the final minute of grilling.
- **Pitta Burgers** Make 8 burgers instead of 4 and serve them in warm pitta bread pockets, with shredded lettuce, chopped cucumber and chopped tomatoes. Add a dollop of Greek yogurt, if liked.

BEEF OLIVES

*This makes an excellent main course for a casual dinner party
and has the advantage that the meat is prepared in individual
portions and needs very little last-minute attention.*

450 g / 1 lb rump or chuck steak, trimmed
45 ml / 3 tbsp dripping or oil
1 large onion, sliced
45 ml / 3 tbsp plain flour
600 ml / 1 pint beef stock
1 tomato, peeled and sliced
1 carrot, sliced
15 ml / 1 tbsp Worcestershire sauce
salt and pepper
30 ml / 2 tbsp chopped parsley
fresh herb sprigs to garnish

STUFFING
50 g / 2 oz margarine
100 g / 4 oz fresh white breadcrumbs
pinch of grated nutmeg
15 ml / 1 tbsp chopped parsley
5 ml / 1 tsp chopped fresh mixed herbs
grated rind of ½ lemon
1 egg, beaten

Make the stuffing. Melt the margarine in a small saucepan. Add the breadcrumbs, nutmeg, herbs and lemon rind, with salt and pepper to taste. Add
enough beaten egg to bind the mixture.

Cut the meat into four slices and flatten each with a cutlet bat or rolling pin.
Divide the stuffing between the meat slices, spreading it out evenly. Roll each
piece of meat up tightly and tie securely with fine string or cotton.

Heat the dripping or oil in a large saucepan and fry the beef olives, turning them
frequently until browned. Using a slotted spoon, transfer them to a plate.

Add the onion slices to the fat remaining in the pan and fry until golden brown. Using a slotted spoon, transfer to the plate with the beef olives. Add the flour to the pan and cook until golden brown, stirring constantly. Gradually add the stock, stirring until the mixture boils, then lower the heat and simmer for 5 minutes.

Return the beef olives and onion slices to the pan. Add the tomato, carrot and Worcestershire sauce, with salt and pepper to taste. Cover the pan with a tight-fitting lid and simmer for 1–2 hours.

Having removed the strings from the beef olives, serve them on a bed of mashed potato or rice. Strain the sauce and pour it over the beef olives. Sprinkle with chopped parsley and garnish with fresh herbs (the same types as used in the stuffing). Serve at once.

SERVES FOUR

VARIATIONS

- **Hanover Rouladen** Omit the stuffing. Instead lay a strip of gherkin on each portion of beef, with 15 ml / 1 tbsp finely chopped onion, 15 ml / 1 tbsp chopped ham and 5 ml / 1 tsp capers. Proceed as in the recipe above but cook for 1½ hours only.
- **Mushroom Paupiettes** Use a mushroom stuffing instead of herb. Chop 1 rindless bacon rasher and fry without additional fat for 2 minutes. Add 100 g / 4 oz finely chopped mushrooms and fry over gentle heat for 5 minutes, stirring. Stir in 100 g / 4 oz fresh white breadcrumbs, a knob of butter and pinch of grated nutmeg. Add salt and pepper to taste. Bind with beaten egg. Prepare and cook the paupiettes as for the beef olives in the recipe above, but stir 250 ml / 8 fl oz soured cream into the sauce just before serving.

CARBONNADE OF BEEF

Brown ale and long, slow cooking combine to make this classic, full-flavoured stew with its crunchy topping of mustard-seasoned French bread.

50 g / 2 oz butter or margarine
675 g / 1½ lb stewing steak, trimmed and cut into 4 cm / 1½ inch cubes
2 large onions, sliced
1 garlic clove, crushed
15 ml / 1 tbsp plain flour
250 ml / 8 fl oz beef stock
375 ml / 13 fl oz brown ale
salt and pepper
1 bouquet garni
pinch of grated nutmeg
pinch of soft light brown sugar
5 ml / 1 tsp red wine vinegar
6 thin slices of French bread
15 ml / 1 tbsp French mustard

Set the oven at 160°C / 325°F / gas 3. Melt the butter or margarine in a heavy-bottomed frying pan, add the beef and fry quickly until browned on all sides. Using a slotted spoon, transfer the beef to a casserole and keep hot. Add the onions to the fat remaining in the pan and fry until lightly browned, then stir in the garlic and fry over gentle heat for 1 minute.

Pour off any excess fat from the pan to leave about 15 ml / 1 tbsp. Add the flour to the onions and garlic and cook, stirring constantly, until lightly browned. Gradually stir in the stock and ale, with salt and pepper to taste. Add the bouquet garni, nutmeg, brown sugar and vinegar. Bring to the boil, then pour the liquid over the beef in the casserole. Cover and bake for 1½–2 hours or until the beef is tender. Remove the bouquet garni.

Spread the French bread slices with mustard. Arrange them, mustard side up, on top of the carbonnade, pressing them down so that they absorb the gravy. Return the casserole to the oven, uncovered, for about 15 minutes or until the bread browns slightly. Alternatively, place under a hot grill for a few minutes. Serve immediately, straight from the casserole.

SERVES SIX

BOLOGNESE SAUCE

15 g / ½ oz butter
15 ml / 1 tbsp olive oil
75 g / 3 oz unsmoked rindless streaky bacon rashers, diced
1 onion, finely chopped
2 garlic cloves, crushed
1 carrot, finely diced
½ celery stick, thinly sliced
225 g / 8 oz lean minced beef
100 g / 4 oz chicken livers, trimmed and cut into small shreds
1 (397 g / 14 oz) can chopped tomatoes
200 ml / 7 fl oz beef stock
15 ml / 1 tbsp tomato purée
125 ml / 4 fl oz dry white or red wine
5 ml / 1 tsp dried marjoram
salt and pepper
pinch of grated nutmeg

Melt the butter in the oil in a saucepan. Add the bacon and cook it gently until brown. Add the onion, garlic, carrot and celery. Cook over gentle heat for about 10 minutes until the onion is soft and just beginning to brown. Add the beef and cook, stirring, until browned and broken up.

Add the chicken livers to the pan and cook for 3 minutes, turning the livers over gently to brown them on all sides. Stir in the tomatoes, stock, tomato purée, wine and marjoram. Add to taste salt, pepper and nutmeg. Bring to simmering point and cook, covered, for about 1 hour, stirring occasionally.

Remove the lid for the final 20 minutes of the cooking time to allow some of the liquid to evaporate. Taste and add extra salt and pepper if necessary. Serve with pasta, rice or baked potatoes.

SERVES FOUR WITH PASTA OR RICE

STEAK PIE

575 g / 1¼ lb chuck or blade steak, trimmed and cut into 1 cm / ½ inch cubes
45 ml / 3 tbsp seasoned flour
2 onions, chopped
about 250 ml / 8 fl oz beef stock
beaten egg or milk for glazing

ROUGH PUFF PASTRY
200 g / 7 oz plain flour
1.25 ml / ¼ tsp salt
150 g / 5 oz butter or half butter, half lard, well chilled
2.5 ml / ½ tsp lemon juice
flour for rolling out

Make the pastry. Sift the flour and salt into a bowl. If butter and lard are used, blend them together evenly with a round-bladed knife and chill. Cut the fat into pieces the size of walnuts and add to the flour. Make a well in the centre, mix in the lemon juice, then gradually add enough cold water to make an elastic dough. On a lightly floured surface, roll into a long strip, keeping the edges square.

Fold the bottom third over the centre third, then fold the top third over. With the rolling pin, press to seal the edges. Turn the pastry so that the folded edges are on the left and right. Repeat the rolling and folding three more times, allowing the pastry to rest in a cool place for 10 minutes between the second and third rollings. Finally, wrap the pastry in foil and store in the refrigerator until required.

In a stout polythene or paper bag, toss the beef cubes in seasoned flour until well coated. Shake off excess flour, then transfer the cubes to a 1 litre / 1¾ pint pie dish, piling them higher in the centre than at the sides and sprinkling chopped onion between the layers. Pour in enough of the stock to quarter-fill the dish. Reserve the remaining stock.

Set the oven at 230°C / 450°F / gas 8. Roll out the pastry on a lightly floured surface. Cut a strip of pastry from around the outside of the piece. Dampen the rim of the pie dish and press the pastry strip on it, trimming off any extra length. Use the remaining pastry to cover the dish. Trim the edge, knock up with the back of a knife and flute the edge. Make a small hole in the centre of the lid and surround it with pastry leaves made from the trimmings. Make a pastry tassel or rose to cover the hole after baking, if liked. Brush the pastry with the beaten egg or milk.

Place the pie on a baking sheet, with the pastry tassel, if made, next to it. Bake for about 10 minutes until the pastry is risen and golden brown. Lower the oven temperature to 180°C / 350°F / gas 4 and, if necessary, move the pie to a lower shelf. Cover loosely with foil to prevent overbrowning and continue to cook for about 2 hours or until the meat is tender when tested through the crust with a skewer.

Heat the reserved beef stock in a small saucepan. Pour it into the pie through a funnel inserted in the hole in the crust. Cover the hole with the pastry tassel or rose, if made, and serve at once.

SERVES SIX

VARIATIONS

- **Steak and Kidney Pie** As above, but add 2 sheep's or 150 g / 5 oz ox kidneys. Skin, core and slice the kidneys before mixing with the steak and onions.
- **Steak and Mushroom Pie** As above, but add 100 g / 4 oz sliced mushrooms to the meat in the pie dish.
- **Steak and Oyster Pie** As above, but add 12 oysters to the meat. Open the oysters and save the liquor from the shells, adding it to the pie.

COTTAGE PIE

50 g / 2 oz butter
575 g / 1¼ lb minced beef
1 onion, chopped
2 carrots, finely chopped
100 g / 4 oz mushrooms, chopped
30 ml / 2 tbsp plain flour
300 ml / ½ pint beef stock
5 ml / 1 tsp Worcestershire sauce
salt and pepper
900 g / 2 lb potatoes, halved
30 ml / 2 tbsp milk
pinch of grated nutmeg

Melt half the butter in a saucepan and fry the minced beef until browned, stirring to break up any lumps. Add the chopped onion, carrots and mushrooms and cook for 10 minutes or until softened slightly.

Stir in the flour, then pour in the beef stock and Worcestershire sauce, with salt and pepper to taste. Bring to the boil, stirring, then cover the pan and simmer for 30 minutes.

Cook the potatoes in a saucepan of salted boiling water for about 20 minutes or until tender. Drain thoroughly and mash with a potato masher. Beat in the remaining butter and the milk to make a creamy consistency. Add salt, pepper and nutmeg to taste.

Set the oven at 200°C / 400°F / gas 6. Spoon the meat mixture into an ovenproof dish. Cover with the potato and mark the top with a fork. Bake for about 25 minutes until the potato topping is browned.

SERVES FOUR TO SIX

CHILLI CON CARNE

225 g / 8 oz red kidney beans, soaked overnight in water to cover
225 g / 8 oz rindless smoked streaky bacon rashers, chopped
1 Spanish onion, chopped
2 garlic cloves, crushed
30 ml / 2 tbsp ground coriander
15 ml / 1 tbsp ground cumin
15 ml / 1 tbsp chili powder (mixed spice powder) or to taste
450 g / 1 lb minced beef
1 beef stock cube
30 ml / 2 tbsp tomato purée
salt and pepper
30 ml / 2 tbsp chopped fresh coriander or parsley

Drain the beans and put them in a large saucepan. Add plenty of water and bring to the boil. Boil vigorously for 10 minutes, then lower the heat, cover the pan and simmer gently for 30 minutes.

Put the bacon in a large heavy-bottomed saucepan. Heat gently until the fat runs. Add the onion and fry, stirring frequently for about 5 minutes until the onion is soft but not browned. Stir in the garlic, ground coriander, cumin and chilli powder. Cook for 1 minute, stirring, then add the meat and cook until lightly browned. Crumble in the stock cube and pour in 600 ml / 1 pint water. Stir in the tomato purée and add salt and pepper to taste. Bring to the boil.

Drain the beans. Add them to the saucepan and bring the stock back to the boil. Cover the pan, lower the heat and simmer gently for about 1 hour or until the beans are tender and the liquid has been absorbed. Stir in the coriander or parsley. Serve at once, with rice, crusty bread or as a filling for baked jacket potatoes.

SERVES FOUR

ROAST RACK OF LAMB

1 rack of lamb
45 ml / 3 tbsp plain flour
salt and pepper
30 ml / 2 tbsp redcurrant jelly

Set the oven at 180°C / 350°F / gas 4. Weigh the joint of lamb and calculate the cooking time at 25 minutes per 450 g / 1 lb, plus 25 minutes. This gives a medium result; for a well-done joint allow 30 minutes per 450 g / 1 lb plus 30 minutes.

Dust the joint with flour and plenty of seasoning. Place it in a roasting tin and cook for three-quarters of the time, basting occasionally. Pour off excess fat and pour in 600 ml / 1 pint boiling water. Finish roasting the meat.

Meanwhile, melt the jelly in a small saucepan. Transfer the meat to a serving plate and glaze it with the jelly. Tent with foil to keep hot. Boil the cooking liquor until reduced by about a third, taste for seasoning, pour into a gravy-boat and serve with the lamb.

SERVES FOUR TO SIX

VARIATIONS

- **Crown Roast or Guard of Honour** A pair of racks of lamb may be trussed into a crown roast or a guard of honour. For a crown, the racks are sewn end to end, then trussed (sewn) into a ring with the fat side inwards and trimmed bones forming the top of the crown. For a guard of honour, the racks are arranged opposite each other with bone ends interlocked. Both joints are sold ready prepared; both may be stuffed. Stuffing is spooned into the middle of the crown roast or packed between the racks for a guard of honour.

LAMB CUTLETS EN PAPILLOTE

oil for greasing
4–6 slices of cooked ham
6 lamb cutlets, trimmed
15 ml / 1 tbsp oil
1 onion, finely chopped
25 g / 1 oz button mushrooms, finely chopped
10 ml / 2 tsp finely chopped parsley
grated rind of ½ lemon
salt and pepper

Set the oven at 190°C / 375°F / gas 5. Cut out 12 small rounds of ham, each large enough to cover the round part of a cutlet. Heat the oil in a small saucepan and fry the onion for 4–6 minutes until slightly softened. Remove from the heat and stir in the mushrooms, parsley and lemon rind, with salt and pepper to taste. Leave to cool.

Cut out six heart-shaped pieces of double thickness greaseproof paper or foil large enough to hold the cutlets. Grease the paper generously with oil. Centre one of the ham rounds on the right half of one of the prepared paper hearts, spread with a little of the mushroom mixture and lay a cutlet on top. Spread the cutlet with a little more of the mushroom mixture and add another round of ham so that the round part of the cutlet is neatly sandwiched. Fold over the paper and twist the edges well together.

Lay the wrapped cutlets on a greased baking sheet and bake for 30 minutes. Transfer, still in their wrappings, to heated individual plates and serve at once.

SERVES SIX

HERBED SHOULDER OF LAMB

This recipe maybe used for leg as well as for shoulder of lamb.

1 shoulder of lamb, boned
4 garlic cloves, peeled and quartered lengthways
about 6 each small fresh rosemary and thyme sprigs
4 bay leaves
2 oranges
60 ml / 4 tbsp olive oil
salt and pepper
300 ml / ½ pint red wine

GARNISH
orange slices
fresh herbs

Trim any lumps of fat from the lamb, then tie it in a neat shape if the butcher has not already done this. Weigh the joint and calculate the cooking time at 30 minutes per 450 g / 1 lb plus 30 minutes. Use a small pointed knife to make short cuts into the lamb, at an angle running under the skin, all over the joint. Insert pieces of garlic and the rosemary and thyme sprigs into the cuts. Place the joint in a deep dish, with two bay leaves underneath and two on top.

Pare two long strips of rind off one orange and add them to the dish, next to or on top of the lamb. Squeeze the juice from the oranges, then mix it with the olive oil, salt and pepper. Pour this mixture over the lamb, cover and marinate for several hours or overnight. Turn the joint at least once during marinating.

Set the oven at 180ºC / 350ºF / gas 4. Transfer the joint to a roasting tin, adding the bay leaves and orange rind but reserving the marinade. Cook for half the calculated time, brushing occasionally with the reserved marinade and basting with cooking juices from the tin. Pour the remaining marinade and the wine over the joint and continue roasting. Baste the lamb occasionally and add a little water to the juices in the tin if they begin to dry up – if the roasting tin is large they will evaporate more speedily.

Transfer the cooked joint to a serving dish, cover with foil and set aside. Pour 300 ml / ½ pint boiling water or vegetable cooking water into the roasting tin.

Boil the cooking juices rapidly, stirring and scraping the sediment off the base and sides of the pan, until they are reduced by half. Taste for seasoning, then strain the sauce into a heated sauceboat.

Garnish the lamb with orange slices and fresh herbs and serve at once, carving it into thick slices. Offer the sauce separately.

SERVES SIX

OXFORD JOHN

**575 g / 1¼ lb boned leg of lamb, trimmed
salt and pepper
15 ml / 1 tbsp finely chopped ham
5 ml / 1 tsp finely chopped onion
5 ml / 1 tsp chopped parsley
2.5 ml / ½ tsp dried mixed herbs
50 g / 2 oz butter or margarine
25 g / 1 oz plain flour
250 ml / 8 fl oz lamb or beef stock
5 ml / 1 tsp lemon juice**

Cut the meat into neat, thin round slices, about 10 cm / 4 inches in diameter. Season with salt and pepper. Put the ham in a bowl and add the onion, herbs and a little salt and pepper. Use this filling to sandwich the rounds of meat together in pairs. Place them on a baking sheet, cover and leave for 1 hour to absorb the flavours.

Melt the butter in a large frying pan and fry the meat 'sandwiches', a few at a time, until browned and cooked. As they cook, transfer the 'sandwiches' to a heated dish; keep hot.

Stir the flour into the fat remaining in the pan and cook until it is well browned. Gradually add the stock, stirring until the mixture boils and thickens. Add the lemon juice and return the meat. Simmer for 10 minutes. Serve hot.

SERVES SIX

MOUSSAKA

fat for greasing
1 aubergine
salt and pepper
30 ml / 2 tbsp olive oil
1 large onion, chopped
1 garlic clove, crushed
450 g / 1 lb minced lamb or beef
10 ml / 2 tsp chopped parsley
2 tomatoes, peeled, seeded and chopped
150 ml / ¼ pint dry white wine
300 ml / ½ pint milk
1 egg, plus 2 egg yolks
pinch of grated nutmeg
75 g / 3 oz Kefalotiri or Parmesan cheese, grated

Grease a 20 x 10 x 10 cm (8 x 4 x 4 inch) baking dish. Set the oven at 180°C / 350°F / gas 4. Cut the aubergine into 1 cm / ½ inch slices, put them in a colander, and sprinkle generously with salt. Set aside.

Heat the olive oil, and gently fry the onion and garlic for about 10 minutes until the onion is soft. Add the mince and continue cooking, stirring with a fork to break up any lumps in the meat. When the meat is thoroughly browned, add salt, pepper, parsley and tomatoes. Mix well, then add the white wine.

In a bowl, beat the milk, whole egg, egg yolks, salt and a good pinch of grated nutmeg together. Add about half the cheese to the egg mixture, then beat again briefly.

Rinse and drain the aubergine slices and pat dry with absorbent kitchen paper. Place half in the bottom of the prepared dish and cover with the meat mixture. Lay the remaining aubergine slices on the meat and pour the milk and egg mixture over them. Sprinkle the remaining cheese on top. Bake for 30–40 minutes, until golden brown.

SERVES FOUR

SHEPHERD'S PIE

butter for greasing
50 g / 2 oz butter
2 onions, roughly chopped
15 ml / 1 tbsp plain flour
250 ml / 8 fl oz well-flavoured lamb stock
575 g / 1¼ lb lean cooked lamb, minced
salt and pepper
5 ml / 1 tsp Worcestershire sauce
675 g / 1½ lb potatoes, halved
15–30 ml / 1–2 tbsp milk
pinch of grated nutmeg

Melt half the butter in a saucepan and fry the onions until softened but not coloured. Stir in the flour and cook gently for 1–2 minutes, stirring all the time. Gradually add the stock. Bring to the boil, stirring until the sauce thickens.

Stir in the lamb, with salt and pepper and Worcestershire sauce to taste. Cover the pan and simmer for 30 minutes.

Meanwhile cook the potatoes in a saucepan of salted boiling water for about 30 minutes or until tender. Drain thoroughly and mash with a potato masher, or beat them with a hand-held electric whisk until smooth. Beat in the rest of the butter and the milk to make a creamy consistency. Add salt, pepper and nutmeg to taste.

Set the oven at 220°C / 450°F / gas 7. Spoon the meat mixture into a greased pie dish or shallow oven-to-table dish. Cover with the potato, smooth the top, then flick it up into small peaks or score a pattern on the surface with a fork. Bake for 10–15 minutes until browned on top. Serve at once.

SERVES FOUR TO SIX

LOIN OF PORK STUFFED WITH PRUNES

1.25–1.5 kg / 2¾–3¼ lb boned loin of pork
200 g / 7 oz ready-to-eat prunes
juice of 1 lemon
salt and pepper

Set the oven at 180°C / 350°F / gas 4. Weigh the meat and calculate the cooking time at 30 minutes per 450 g / 1 lb plus 30 minutes over. Spread the prunes over the pork flesh, roll up meat and tie it securely. Pour the lemon juice all over the meat, rubbing it well in.

Put the meat in a roasting tin, season with salt and pepper and roast for the calculated cooking time, basting occasionally. Serve on a heated platter, accompanied with a thickened gravy made from the sediment in the roasting tin (see pages 238–9).

SERVES SIX

HAM AND EGGS

4 gammon steaks
4 eggs

Trim the rind from the gammon steaks. Put it in a large cold frying pan. Heat, gently at first, until the fat runs, pressing the rind to extract the fat. Tilt the pan to grease it thoroughly, then discard the rind.

Snip the fat around the gammon steaks at intervals, add them to the pan and cook for about 20 minutes, turning several times.

Using tongs, transfer the gammon to a heated platter. Fry the eggs in the fat remaining in the pan, spooning the fat over the top from time to time until the whites are firm and yolks set. Alternatively, poach the eggs. Serve on top of the ham.

SERVES FOUR

ROAST PORK WITH SAGE AND ONION STUFFING

*Use the pan juices from the pork to make a gravy
and offer Apple Sauce (page 240) as an accompaniment.*

4 large onions
100 g / 4 oz fresh breadcrumbs
45 ml / 3 tbsp chopped fresh sage or 15 ml / 1 tbsp dried sage
salt and pepper
40 g / 1½ oz butter, melted
1 egg
1. 5 kg / 3 lb boned joint from leg of pork, boned and scored
30 ml / 2 tbsp oil

Place the onions in a saucepan, cover with water and bring to the boil. Cook for 5 minutes, then drain, cool slightly and chop. Mix the onions with the breadcrumbs. Add the sage, plenty of seasoning, the butter and the egg.

Set the oven at 180°C / 350°F / gas 4. Make sure the pork rind is well scored. Fill the cavity left by the bone with some stuffing, then tie the joint into a neat shape. Place the remaining stuffing in a buttered, ovenproof dish; set aside.

Place the joint in a roasting tin and rub plenty of salt into the rind, then trickle the oil over. Roast for about 2 hours, basting the joint occasionally, until cooked through. Place the dish of stuffing in the oven halfway through cooking.

SERVES SIX

CIDERED PORK CHOPS

4 pork loin chops, trimmed
oil (optional)
60 ml / 4 tbsp dry cider
1 bouquet garni
2 cooking apples
2 onions, chopped
pinch of ground cinnamon
salt and pepper
100 g / 4 oz flat mushrooms, thickly sliced
200 g / 7 oz fresh peas
25 g / 1 oz butter
200 g / 7 oz cooked small whole beetroot
225 g / 8 oz tagliatelle, cooked

Set the oven at 160°C / 325°F / gas 3. Heat a frying pan. Brown the chops on both sides, adding a little oil if the chops are very lean. Remove the chops and place them in a casserole. Pour the cider over the chops and add the bouquet garni. Cover the casserole and start cooking it in the oven.

Peel, core and chop the apples. Add them with the onions to the fat remaining in the frying pan and fry gently for 5 minutes. Stir in the cinnamon, with just enough water to cover the onion mixture. Cover the pan and simmer for about 15 minutes, until the onions and apples are soft. Rub the mixture through a sieve into a bowl, add salt and pepper to taste, then spoon the mixture over the chops in the casserole. Return to the oven for 45 minutes.

Add the mushrooms and peas to the casserole and cook for 30 minutes more. Towards the end of the cooking time, melt the butter in a small saucepan, add the beetroot and heat gently, turning often. Arrange the tagliatelle and chops on a heated serving dish with the chops on top. Arrange the mushrooms, peas and beetroot around them.

SERVES FOUR

TOAD-IN-THE-HOLE

450 g / 1 lb pork sausages

BATTER
100 g / 4 oz plain flour
1.25 ml / ¼ tsp salt
1 egg beaten
300 ml / ½ pint milk, or milk and water

Make the batter. Sift the flour and salt into a bowl, make a well in the centre and add the beaten egg. Stir in half the milk (or all the milk, if using a mixture of milk and water), gradually working in the flour.

Beat vigorously until the mixture is smooth and bubbly, then stir in the rest of the milk (or the water). Pour the batter into a jug and set aside.

Set the oven at 220°C / 425°F / gas 7. Arrange the sausages, spoke-fashion, in a shallow 1.1 litre / 2 pint circular dish. Stand the dish on a baking sheet and cook the sausages for 15 minutes.

Pour the batter over the sausages and bake for 40–45 minutes more until golden brown and well risen. Serve at once with a rich gravy or home-made tomato sauce.

SERVES FOUR

MEATLOAF

oil for greasing
450 g / 1 lb minced beef or pork, or a mixture of both
50 g / 2 oz fresh breadcrumbs
1 large onion, finely chopped
15ml / 2 tbsp chopped parsley
5 ml / 1 tsp chopped fresh thyme
5 ml / 1 tsp chopped fresh sage
1 egg
15 ml / 1 tbsp Worcestershire sauce
salt and pepper

Grease a 450 g / 1 lb loaf tin. Set the oven at 180ºC / 350ºF / gas 4. Place all the ingredients in a bowl, adding plenty of salt and pepper. Pound the ingredients with the back of a mixing spoon until thoroughly combined and well bound together.

Turn the mixture into the tin, press it down well and cover the top with a piece of greased greaseproof paper. Bake for 1 hour, until firm and shrunk away from the tin slightly. Turn out and serve hot or cold.

SERVES FOUR

Vegetables

*An inspiring collection of vibrant
vegetable side-dishes including
garlanded asparagus and carrots in cider,
comforting potato recipes, plus
substantial vegetarian main courses.*

GARLANDED ASPARAGUS

30 asparagus spears
75 g / 3 oz butter
salt and pepper
50 g / 2 oz Parmesan cheese, grated
4 egg yolks, unbroken
butter for frying

Set the oven at 200°C / 400°F / gas 6. Prepare and steam the asparagus for 3 minutes. Dry thoroughly and place in an ovenproof dish. Melt half the butter in a small frying pan and spoon it over the top. Sprinkle with salt and pepper to taste and top with the Parmesan. Bake for 15 minutes or until the topping is golden brown.

Meanwhile, add the remaining butter to the frying pan and melt over gentle heat. Add the egg yolks, taking care not to break them, and cook gently until just set outside, basting often. Using an egg slice, carefully lift them out of the pan, draining off excess fat, and arrange them around the asparagus. Serve at once.

SERVES FOUR

FRIED AUBERGINES WITH ONION

2 aubergines
salt and pepper
50 g / 2 oz plain flour
cayenne pepper
oil for frying
1 onion, finely chopped
30 ml / 2 tbsp chopped parsley to garnish

Cut the ends off the aubergines, slice them thinly and put them in a colander. Sprinkle generously with salt. Set aside for 30 minutes, then rinse, drain and dry thoroughly on absorbent kitchen paper.

Mix the flour with a pinch each of salt and cayenne. Add the aubergine slices, toss until lightly coated, then shake off excess flour.

Heat a little oil in a large frying pan, add the onion and cook over moderate heat for about 10 minutes until golden. Using a slotted spoon, transfer to a small bowl and keep hot.

Add the aubergine slices, a few at a time, to the hot oil in the pan. Fry until soft and lightly browned, turning once during cooking. As the slices brown, remove them from the pan with a fish slice, arrange on a heated serving dish and keep hot. Add extra oil and heat it as necessary between batches of aubergine slices.

When all the aubergine slices have been fried, sprinkle them with the fried onion and the chopped parsley. Serve at once.

SERVES SIX

BEANS WITH SOURED CREAM

fat for greasing
450 g / 1 lb runner beans
150 ml / ¼ pint soured cream
1.25 ml / ¼ tsp grated nutmeg
1.25 ml / ¼ tsp caraway seeds
salt and pepper
50 g / 2 oz butter
50 g / 2 oz fresh white breadcrumbs

Set the oven at 200°C / 400°F / gas 6. Grease a 1 litre / 1¾ pint baking dish. Wash the beans, string them if necessary and slice them thinly. Cook in boiling water for 3–7 minutes until cooked to taste. Alternatively, cook in a steamer over boiling water. Drain thoroughly.

Combine the soured cream, nutmeg and caraway seeds in a bowl. Stir in salt and pepper to taste. Add the beans and toss well together. Spoon the mixture into the baking dish.

Melt the butter in a small frying pan, add the breadcrumbs and fry over gentle heat for 2–3 minutes. Sprinkle the mixture over the beans. Bake for 20–30 minutes or until the topping is crisp and golden.

SERVES THREE TO FOUR

MICROWAVE TIP

The first stage of this recipe – cooking the runner beans – may be done in the microwave. Put the beans in a dish with 60 ml / 4 tbsp water. Cover loosely and cook on High for 10–12 minutes, stirring once or twice. Take care when removing the cover to avoid being scalded by the steam.

BROAD BEANS
WITH CREAM SAUCE

250 ml / 8 fl oz chicken stock
15 ml / 1 tbsp chopped fresh herbs (parsley, thyme, sage, savory)
1 kg / 2¼ lb broad beans, shelled
1 egg yolk
150 ml / ¼ pint single cream
salt and pepper

Combine the stock and herbs in a saucepan. Bring to the boil, add the beans and cook for 5–15 minutes until tender. Lower the heat to a bare simmer.

Beat the egg yolk with the cream in a small bowl. Add 30 ml / 2 tbsp of the hot stock and mix well, then pour the contents of the bowl into the pan. Heat gently, stirring all the time, until the sauce thickens slightly. Do not allow the mixture to boil or it will curdle. Add salt and pepper to taste and serve.

SERVES FOUR

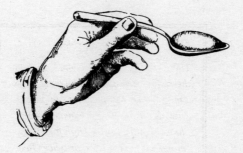

BAVARIAN CABBAGE

75 g / 3 oz butter
1 onion, finely chopped
1.1 kg / 2½ lb white cabbage, washed, quartered and shredded
1 cooking apple
salt and pepper
10 ml / 2 tsp sugar
125 ml / 4 fl oz vegetable stock or water
1.25 ml / ¼ tsp caraway seeds
15 ml / 1 tbsp cornflour
60 ml / 4 tbsp white wine

Melt the butter in a heavy-bottomed saucepan. Add the onion and fry gently for 10 minutes until soft but not coloured. Stir in the cabbage, tossing it lightly in the fat.

Peel and core the apple, chop it finely and stir it into the pan. Add salt and pepper to taste, then stir in the sugar, stock or water, and caraway seeds. Cover the pan with a tight-fitting lid and simmer very gently for 1 hour.

Meanwhile mix the cornflour and wine together in a small bowl. Stir the mixture into the pan. Bring to the boil, stirring the mixture constantly until it thickens. Cook for 2–3 minutes, still stirring. Serve at once.

SERVES SIX

VARIATION

- For a slightly more fruity flavour, increase the number of apples to 2 and substitute cider for the stock and wine. Omit the caraway seeds.

RED CABBAGE WITH APPLES

45 ml / 3 tbsp oil
1 onion, finely chopped
1 garlic clove, crushed
900 g / 2 lb red cabbage, finely shredded
2 large cooking apples
15 ml / 1 tbsp soft light brown sugar or golden syrup
· juice of ½ lemon
30 ml / 2 tbsp red wine vinegar
salt and pepper
· 15 ml / 1 tbsp caraway seeds (optional)

Heat the oil in a large saucepan, add the onion and garlic and fry gently for 5 minutes. Add the cabbage. Peel, core and slice the apples and add them to the pan with the sugar or syrup. Cook over very gentle heat for 10 minutes, shaking the pan frequently.

Add the lemon juice and vinegar, with salt and pepper to taste. Stir in the caraway seeds, if used. Cover and simmer gently for 1–1½ hours, stirring occasionally and adding a little water if the mixture appears dry. Check the seasoning before serving.

SERVES SIX

CARROTS WITH CIDER

*This traditional way of cooking carrots was
originally known as the 'conservation method' because
it preserved as many of the nutrients as possible.*

75 g / 3 oz butter
675 g / 1½ lb young carrots, trimmed and scraped
salt
60 ml / 4 tbsp double cream
125 ml / 4 fl oz dry cider
few drops of lemon juice
pepper

Melt 25 g / 1 oz of the butter in a heavy-bottomed saucepan. Add the carrots and cook over very gentle heat for 10 minutes, shaking the pan frequently so that the carrots do not stick to the base. Pour over 100 ml / 3½ fl oz boiling water, with salt to taste. Cover the pan and simmer the carrots for about 10 minutes more or until tender. Drain, reserving the liquid for use in soup or stock.

Melt the remaining butter in the clean pan. Gradually stir in the cream and cider. Add the lemon juice and salt and pepper to taste. Stir in the carrots, cover the pan and cook gently for 10 minutes more. Serve at once.

SERVES SIX

CAULIFLOWER CHEESE

salt and pepper
1 firm cauliflower
30 ml / 2 tbsp butter
60 ml / 4 tbsp plain flour
200 ml / 7 fl oz milk
125 g / 4½ oz Cheddar cheese, grated
pinch of dry mustard
pinch of cayenne pepper
25 g / 1 oz dried white breadcrumbs

Bring a saucepan of salted water to the boil, add the cauliflower, cover the pan and cook gently for 20–30 minutes until tender. Drain well, reserving 175 ml / 6 fl oz of the cooking water. Leave the cauliflower head whole or cut carefully into florets. Place in a warmed ovenproof dish, cover with greased greaseproof paper and keep hot.

Set the oven at 220°C / 425°F / gas 7 or preheat the grill. Melt the butter in a saucepan, stir in the flour and cook for 1 minute. Gradually add the milk and reserved cooking water, stirring all the time until the sauce boils and thickens. Remove from the heat and stir in 100 g / 4 oz of the cheese, stirring until it melts into the sauce. Add the mustard and cayenne, with salt and pepper to taste.

Pour the sauce over the cauliflower. Mix the remaining cheese with the breadcrumbs and sprinkle them on top. Brown the topping for 7–10 minutes in the oven or under the grill. Serve at once.

SERVES FOUR

COURGETTES WITH DILL

A simple dish to go with fish.

25 g / 1 oz butter
grated rind of ½ lemon
8 small courgettes, trimmed and sliced
salt and pepper
45 ml / 3 tbsp chopped fresh dill
squeeze of lemon juice

Melt the butter in a large frying pan. Add the lemon rind and cook for a few seconds, then add the courgettes. Cook over medium to high heat for 2–3 minutes, add salt and pepper, and dill. Toss in a little lemon juice and serve.

SERVES FOUR

COURGETTES WITH ALMONDS

The cooked courgettes should be firm and full flavoured,
not overcooked and watery.

25 g / 1 oz butter
25 g / 1 oz blanched almonds, split in half
450 g / 1 lb courgettes, trimmed and thinly sliced
salt and pepper
30 ml / 2 tbsp snipped chives or chopped parsley

Melt the butter in a large frying pan. Add the almonds and fry over moderate heat, stirring, until lightly browned. Tip the courgettes into the pan and cook, gently stirring and turning the slices all the time, for 3–5 minutes.

Tip the courgettes into a heated serving dish, add salt and pepper to taste and sprinkle the chives or parsley over them. Serve at once.

SERVES FOUR TO SIX

FENNEL WITH LEEKS

4 fennel bulbs, trimmed and halved
juice of ½ lemon
knob of butter or 30 ml / 2 tbsp olive oil
4 leeks, sliced
1 bay leaf
2 fresh thyme sprigs
salt and pepper
150 ml / ¼ pint chicken or vegetable stock
45 ml / 3 tbsp dry sherry (optional)

Set the oven at 180°C / 350°F / gas 4. As soon as the fennel is prepared, sprinkle the lemon juice over the cut bulbs. Heat the butter or oil in a frying pan and sauté the leeks for 2 minutes to soften them slightly. Add the pieces of fennel to the pan, pushing the leeks to one side. Turn the pieces of fennel in the fat for a minute or so, then tip the contents of the pan into an ovenproof casserole.

Add the bay leaf and thyme to the vegetables and sprinkle in salt and pepper to taste. Pour the stock and sherry (if used) over the fennel and cover the dish. Bake for 1–1¼ hours, turning the fennel mixture over twice, until tender. Taste for seasoning, remove the bay leaf and serve.

SERVES FOUR

BUTTERED LEEKS

50 g / 2 oz butter
675 g / 1½ lb leeks, trimmed, sliced and washed
15 ml / 1 tbsp lemon juice
salt and pepper
30 ml / 2 tbsp single cream (optional)

Melt the butter in a heavy-bottomed saucepan. Add the leeks and lemon juice, with salt and pepper to taste. Cover the pan and cook the leeks over very gentle heat for about 30 minutes or until very tender. Shake the pan from time to time to prevent the leeks from sticking to the base. Serve in the cooking liquid. Stir in the cream when serving, if liked.

SERVES FOUR

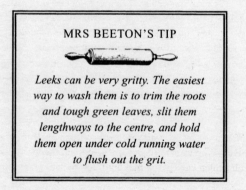

MRS BEETON'S TIP

Leeks can be very gritty. The easiest way to wash them is to trim the roots and tough green leaves, slit them lengthways to the centre, and hold them open under cold running water to flush out the grit.

BAKED STUFFED MARROW

fat for greasing
1 marrow
1 small onion, finely chopped or grated
225 g / 8 oz minced beef
100 g / 4 oz pork sausagemeat or 100 g / 4 oz extra minced beef
25 g / 1 oz fresh white breadcrumbs
15 ml / 1 tbsp chopped parsley
15 ml / 1 tbsp snipped chives
5 ml / 1 tsp Worcestershire sauce
salt and pepper
1 egg, beaten

SAUCE
25 g / 1 oz butter
25 g / 1 oz plain flour
300 ml / ½ pint milk, stock or mixture (see method)
75–100 g / 3–4 oz Cheddar cheese, grated
pinch of dry mustard

Generously grease a large, shallow casserole. Set the oven at 180ºC / 350ºF / gas 4. Halve the marrow lengthways and scoop out the seeds. Lay the halves side by side in the prepared casserole.

Put the onion into a bowl with the beef, sausagemeat, if used, breadcrumbs, parsley, chives, Worcestershire sauce and salt and pepper. Mix well. Bind the mixture with beaten egg. Avoid making it too moist.

Divide the stuffing between each marrow half. Cover the dish and bake for 1 hour.

Strain off most of the liquid in the casserole. Meanwhile make the sauce. Melt the butter in a saucepan. Stir in the flour and cook over low heat for 2–3 minutes, without colouring. Over very low heat, gradually add the liquid (the casserole juices may be used), stirring constantly. Bring to the boil, stirring, then lower the heat and simmer for 1–2 minutes until smooth and thickened. Add the cheese, mustard and salt and pepper to taste. Pour the cheese sauce over the marrow and bake, uncovered, for a further 20 minutes, until the sauce topping is golden brown.

SERVES FOUR TO SIX

MUSHROOMS IN CREAM SAUCE

50 g / 2 oz butter
450 g / 1 lb small button mushrooms
10 ml / 2 tsp arrowroot
125 ml / 4 fl oz chicken or vegetable stock
15 ml / 1 tbsp lemon juice
30 ml / 2 tbsp double cream
salt and pepper
30 ml / 2 tbsp chopped parsley

Melt the butter in large frying pan, add the mushrooms and fry over gentle heat without browning for 10 minutes.

Put the arrowroot in a small bowl. Stir in 30 ml / 2 tbsp of the stock until smooth. Add the remaining stock to the mushrooms and bring to the boil. Lower the heat and simmer gently for 15 minutes, stirring occasionally. Stir in the arrowroot, bring to the boil, stirring, then remove the pan from the heat.

Stir in the lemon juice and cream, with salt and pepper to taste. Serve sprinkled with parsley.

SERVES FOUR TO SIX

MUSHROOMS WITH BACON AND WINE

6 rindless streaky bacon rashers, chopped
400 g / 14 oz button mushrooms, halved or quartered if large
5 ml / 1 tsp snipped chives
5 ml / 1 tsp chopped parsley
10 ml / 2 tsp plain flour
75 ml / 5 tbsp white wine or cider
salt and pepper

Cook the bacon gently in a heavy-bottomed saucepan until the fat begins to run, then increase the heat to moderate and fry for 10 minutes. Add the mushrooms and herbs, tossing them in the bacon fat.

Sprinkle the flour over the mushrooms, cook for 1 minute, stirring gently, then add the wine or cider. Simmer for 10 minutes, stirring occasionally. Season and serve.

SERVES SIX

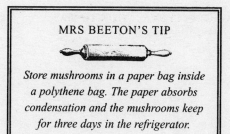

MRS BEETON'S TIP

Store mushrooms in a paper bag inside a polythene bag. The paper absorbs condensation and the mushrooms keep for three days in the refrigerator.

GLAZED ONIONS

Glazed onions make a tasty accompaniment to grilled steak, baked ham or bacon chops. They are often used as a garnish.

400 g / 14 oz button onions
chicken stock (see method)
salt and pepper
15 ml / 1 tbsp soft light brown sugar
25 g / 1 oz butter
pinch of grated nutmeg

Skin the onions and put them in a single layer in a large saucepan. Add just enough stock to cover. Bring to a simmering point and cook for 15–20 minutes until the onions are just tender, adding a small amount of extra stock if necessary.

By the time the onions are cooked, the stock should have reduced almost to a glaze. Remove from the heat and stir in the remaining ingredients. Turn the onions over with a spoon so that the added ingredients mix well and the onions are coated in the mixture.

Return the pan to the heat until the onions become golden and glazed. Serve at once, with the remaining syrupy glaze.

SERVES FOUR

VARIATION

- **Citrus Glazed Onions** Melt 25 g / 1 oz butter in a frying pan. Add 400 g / 14 oz button onions. Sprinkle with 15 ml / 1 tbsp soft light brown sugar. Add salt and pepper to taste and fry, turning the onions occasionally until golden brown. Stir in 150 ml / ¼ pint orange juice and 10 ml / 2 tsp lemon juice. Cover and simmer for 15 minutes.

PANFRIED ONION AND APPLE

40 g / 1½ oz butter
350 g / 12 oz onions, sliced in rings
450 g / 1 lb cooking apples
10 ml / 2 tsp caster sugar
salt and pepper

Melt the butter in a heavy-bottomed frying pan. Add the onions and fry gently. Peel, core and slice the apples into the pan. Mix lightly to coat the apples in the melted butter. Sprinkle the sugar over the top, cover and simmer for 30 minutes or until the onions and apples are tender. Add salt and pepper to taste.

SERVES FOUR

CREAMED ONIONS

fat for greasing
1 kg / 2¼ lb small onions, peeled but left whole
100 ml / 3½ fl oz double cream
Béchamel sauce (page 232) made using 300 ml / ½ pint milk
grated nutmeg
salt and pepper
25 g / 1 oz butter
50 g / 2 oz dried white breadcrumbs
30 ml / 2 tbsp chopped parsley

Grease a 1 litre / 1¾ pint casserole. Set the oven at 160°C / 325°F / gas 3. Bring a saucepan of water to the boil. Add the onions and cook for 10–15 minutes until just tender. Drain well.

Add the double cream to the Béchamel sauce and reheat gently without boiling. Stir in the nutmeg with salt and pepper to taste, add the onions and mix lightly.

Spoon the mixture into the prepared casserole. Top with the breadcrumbs and dot with the butter. Bake for 20 minutes. Serve hot, sprinkled with the parsley.

SERVES SIX TO EIGHT

PETITS POIS A LA FRANCAISE

50 g / 2 oz butter
1 lettuce heart, shredded
1 bunch of spring onions, finely chopped
675 g / 1½ lb fresh shelled garden peas or frozen petits pois
pinch of sugar
salt and pepper

Melt the butter in a heavy-bottomed saucepan and add the lettuce, spring onions, peas and sugar, with salt and pepper to taste. Cover and simmer very gently until the peas are tender. Frozen petits pois may be ready in less than 10 minutes, but fresh garden peas could take as much as 25 minutes.

SERVES SIX

SHERRIED MUSHROOMS

25 g / 1 oz butter
30 ml / 2 tbsp plain flour
250 ml / 8 fl oz milk
45 ml / 3 tbsp dry sherry
350 g / 12 oz mushrooms, sliced
salt and pepper
toast triangles to serve

Melt the butter in a saucepan, add the flour and cook for 1 minute. Gradually add the milk, stirring all the time until the mixture boils and thickens.

Stir in the sherry, then add the mushrooms, with salt and pepper to taste. Cook over gentle heat, stirring frequently, for about 5 minutes or until the mushrooms are just cooked.

Spoon on to a heated serving dish and serve at once, with toast triangles.

SERVES FOUR TO SIX

PEPERONATA

*A delicious starter from Italy, peperonata is perfect for serving
with prosciutto or salami.*

45 ml / 3 tbsp olive oil
1 large onion, sliced
2 garlic cloves, crushed
350 g / 12 oz tomatoes, peeled, seeded and cut in quarters
2 large red peppers, seeded and cut in thin strips
1 large green pepper, seeded and cut in thin strips
1 large yellow pepper, seeded and cut in thin strips
2.5 ml / ½ tsp coriander seeds, lightly crushed (optional)
salt and pepper
15 ml / 1 tbsp red wine vinegar (optional)

Heat the oil in a large frying pan, add the onion and garlic and fry over gentle
heat for 10 minutes. Add the tomatoes, peppers and coriander seeds, if used,
with salt and pepper to taste. Cover and cook gently for 1 hour, stirring from
time to time. Add more salt and pepper before serving if necessary. To sharpen
the flavour, stir in the red wine vinegar, if liked.

SERVES FOUR

POTATOES LYONNAISE

This is a very good way of using up leftover boiled new potatoes.
A crushed garlic clove may be added to the onion, if liked.

1 kg / 2¼ lb potatoes, scrubbed but not peeled
75 g / 3 oz butter or margarine
225 g / 8 oz onions, thickly sliced
salt and pepper
15 ml / 1 tbsp chopped parsley

Boil or steam the potatoes in their jackets until tender. When cool enough to handle, peel and cut into slices 5 mm / ¼ inch thick.

Melt the butter or margarine in a large frying pan. Add the onions and fry over moderate heat until just golden. Using a slotted spoon, transfer the onions to a plate; keep warm. Add the potatoes to the fat remaining in the pan and fry on both sides until crisp and golden.

Return the onions to the pan and mix with the potatoes. Add salt and pepper to taste, turn into a serving dish and sprinkle with the parsley.

SERVES SIX

DUCHESSE POTATOES

**butter or margarine for greasing
450 g / 1 lb old potatoes
salt and pepper
25 g / 1 oz butter or margarine
1 egg or 2 egg yolks
grated nutmeg (optional)
beaten egg for brushing**

Grease a baking sheet. Cut the potatoes into pieces and cook in a saucepan of salted water for 15–20 minutes. Drain thoroughly, then press the potatoes through a sieve into a large mixing bowl.

Set the oven at 200°C / 400°F / gas 6. Beat the butter or margarine and egg or egg yolks into the potatoes. Add salt and pepper to taste and the nutmeg, if used. Spoon the mixture into a piping bag fitted with a large rose nozzle. Pipe rounds of potato on to the prepared baking sheet. Brush with a little beaten egg. Bake for about 15 minutes, until golden brown.

SERVES SIX

GRATIN DAUPHINOIS

25 g / 1 oz butter
1 kg / 2¼ lb, potatoes, thinly sliced
1 large onion, about 200 g / 7 oz, thinly sliced
200 g / 7 oz Gruyère cheese, grated
salt and pepper
grated nutmeg
125 ml / 4 fl oz single cream

Butter a 1.5 litre / 2¾ pint casserole, reserving the remaining butter. Set the oven at 190°C / 375°F / gas 5. Bring a saucepan of water to the boil, add the potatoes and onion, then blanch for 30 seconds. Drain.

Put a layer of potatoes in the bottom of the prepared casserole. Dot with a little of the butter, then sprinkle with some of the onion and cheese, a little salt, pepper and grated nutmeg. Pour over some of the cream. Repeat the layers until all the ingredients have been used, finishing with a layer of cheese. Pour the remaining cream on top.

Cover and bake for 1 hour. Remove from the oven and place under a hot grill for 5 minutes, until the top of the cheese is golden brown and bubbling.

SERVES SIX

POTATOES SAVOYARDE

1 small garlic clove, cut in half
75 g / 3 oz Gruyère cheese, grated
1 kg / 2¼ lb potatoes, thinly sliced
salt and pepper
freshly grated nutmeg
40 g / 1½ oz butter
about 375 ml / 13 fl oz chicken or vegetable stock

Set the oven at 190ºC / 375ºF / gas 5. Rub the cut garlic all over the inside of a 2 litre / 3½ pint baking dish. Set aside 30 ml / 2 tbsp of the grated cheese.

Put the potatoes into a mixing bowl. Add salt, pepper and a little nutmeg to taste, then mix in the remaining cheese. Use a little of the butter to grease the baking dish generously, add the potato mixture and pour in just enough stock to cover the potatoes.

Dot the remaining butter over the potatoes and sprinkle with the reserved grated cheese. Bake for 1¼ hours or until golden brown and the potatoes are tender.

SERVES SIX

BAKED JACKET POTATOES

4 large, even-sized baking potatoes
oil for brushing (optional)
butter or flavoured butter, to serve

Set the oven at 200°C / 400°F / gas 6. Scrub the potatoes, dry them with absorbent kitchen paper and pierce the skin several times with a skewer. If you like soft jackets, brush the potatoes all over with oil.

Bake the potatoes directly on the oven shelf for 1–1½ hours. Test by pressing gently with the fingers. To serve, cut a cross in the top of each potato with a sharp knife. Squeeze the sides of the potato so that the top opens up. Add a pat of plain or flavoured butter and serve.

SERVES FOUR

FILLINGS

Make a meal of baked jacket potatoes by cutting them in half, scooping out the centres and mashing them with selected ingredients. Pile the fillings back into the potato shells and heat through, if necessary, in a 180°C / 350°F / gas 4 oven for about 20 minutes. Alternatively, reheat in the microwave oven or under a moderate grill.

- **Cheese and Ham** Mash the potato. Grate in 100 g / 4 oz Cheddar cheese, add 50 g / 2 oz chopped ham (use trimmings for economy) and mix with 25 g / 1 oz softened butter. Replace in oven until golden.
- **Kipper** Mash the potato with 75 g / 3 oz flaked cooked kipper. Add 1 chopped hard-boiled egg, with salt and pepper to taste. Thin with a little milk, if necessary. Reheat.
- **Frankfurter** Mash the potato with butter. For each potato, add 2 heated chopped frankfurters and 15 ml / 1 tbsp tomato relish. Add chopped parsley.

MICROWAVE TIP

Cooking jacket potatoes in the microwave has practically become a national pastime. Prick the potatoes several times with a skewer or they may burst. Cook directly on the microwave rack or wrap in absorbent kitchen paper if a very soft potato is preferred. For crisper potatoes, brush with oil or butter after microwave cooking, then crisp under a hot grill, turning once. Jacket potatoes also cook extremely well in a combination microwave oven. Follow the instructions in your handbook.

MICROWAVE COOKING TIMES ON HIGH
(600–650 WATT OVENS)

Large potatoes (350 g / 12 oz)

1 potato	8 minutes
2 potatoes	15 minutes
4 potatoes	27 minutes

Medium potatoes (150 g / 5 oz)

1 potato	4 minutes
2 potatoes	5–6 minutes
4 potatoes	10 minutes
6 potatoes	18–19 minutes

TOPPINGS

The easy option. Cut the potatoes almost but not quite in half and open out. Top with any of the mixtures suggested below.

• **Blue Cheese and Yogurt Mash** 100 g / 4 oz ripe Danish blue cheese. Mix with 150 ml / ¼ pint Greek yogurt.
• **Sausage and Chutney** Mix hot or cold sliced cooked sausage with diced eating apple, chopped spring onions and a little of your favourite chutney.
• **Egg Mayonnaise** Mash hard-boiled eggs with a little mayonnaise or plain

yogurt. Add 5 ml / 1 tsp tomato ketchup or tomato purée and some snipped chives.

- **Sardine** Mash canned sardines in tomato sauce and mix with diced cucumber. Serve with shredded lettuce.

- **Chick-pea Mash** 100 g / 4 oz drained canned chick-peas. Mix with 1 crushed garlic clove and 15–30 ml / 1–2 tbsp Greek yogurt. Top with chopped spring onion and sesame seeds.

- **Cheese Soufflé** Combine 100 g / 4 oz grated Cheddar cheese and 1 beaten egg. Cut potatoes in half, pile some of the mixture on each half and grill until topping puffs up and turns golden brown.

- **Peas and Bacon** Combine 100 g / 4 oz cooked petits pois and 3 crumbled grilled rindless bacon rashers. Top with a knob of butter.

- **Broccoli and Asparagus** Mix 175 g / 6 oz cooked broccoli and 100 g / 4 oz drained canned asparagus tips. Stir in 150 ml / ¼ pint soured cream, with salt and pepper to taste.

- **Southern Special** Warm 100–150 g / 4–5 oz creamed sweetcorn. Spoon on to potatoes. Top each portion with 2 grilled rindless bacon rashers and 3–4 banana slices.

ITALIAN SPINACH

25 g / 1 oz sultanas
1 kg / 2¼ lb spinach
30 ml / 2 tbsp oil
1 garlic clove, crushed
salt and pepper
25 g / 1 oz pine nuts

Put the sultanas in a small bowl or mug, pour on boiling water to cover and set aside for 2–3 minutes until plumped. Drain well and set the sultanas aside.

Wash the fresh spinach several times and remove any coarse stalks. Put into a saucepan with just the water that clings to the leaves, then cover the pan. Put the pan over high heat for 2–3 minutes, shaking it frequently. Lower the heat, stir the spinach and cook for a further 5 minutes, turning the spinach occasionally, until cooked to your liking. Drain thoroughly, then chop the spinach coarsely.

Heat the oil in a large frying pan. Add the spinach and garlic, with salt and pepper to taste. Turn the spinach over and over in the pan with a wide spatula to heat it thoroughly without frying. Turn into a heated serving bowl, add the sultanas and nuts and mix lightly. Serve at once.

SERVES FOUR

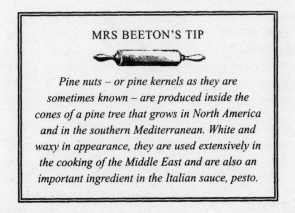

MRS BEETON'S TIP

*Pine nuts – or pine kernels as they are
sometimes known – are produced inside the
cones of a pine tree that grows in North America
and in the southern Mediterranean. White and
waxy in appearance, they are used extensively in
the cooking of the Middle East and are also an
important ingredient in the Italian sauce, pesto.*

RATATOUILLE

Traditionally, the vegetable mixture is cooked gently for about 45–60 minutes and it is richer, and more intensely flavoured if prepared ahead, cooled and thoroughly reheated. This recipe suggests cooking for slightly less time, so that the courgettes and aubergines still retain a bit of bite; the final simmering time may be shortened, if liked, to give a mixture in which the courgettes contribute a slightly crunchy texture.

**2 aubergines,
salt and pepper
125–150 ml / 4–5 fl oz olive oil
2 large onions, finely chopped
2 garlic cloves, crushed
2 peppers, seeded and cut into thin strips
30 ml / 2 tbsp chopped fresh marjoram or 10 ml / 2 tsp dried marjoram
450 g / 1 lb tomatoes, peeled and chopped
4 courgettes, thinly sliced
30 ml / 2 tbsp finely chopped parsley or mint**

Cut the ends off the aubergines and cut them into cubes. Put the cubes in a colander and sprinkle generously with salt. Set aside for 30 minutes, then rinse thoroughly, drain and pat dry on absorbent kitchen paper.

Heat some of the oil in a large saucepan or flameproof casserole, add some of the aubergine cubes and cook over moderate heat, stirring frequently, for 10 minutes. Using a slotted spoon, transfer the aubergine to a bowl; repeat until all the cubes are cooked, adding more oil as necessary. Add the onions to the oil remaining in the pan and fry for 5 minutes, until slightly softened. Stir in the garlic, peppers and marjoram, with salt and pepper to taste. Cook, stirring occasionally for 15–20 minutes, or until the onions are thoroughly softened.

Stir the tomatoes and courgettes into the vegetable mixture. Replace the aubergines, heat until bubbling, then cover and simmer for a further 15–20 minutes, stirring occasionally. Serve hot with parsley, or cold with mint.

SERVES FOUR TO SIX

VEGETABLE CHILLI

1 large aubergine, trimmed and cut into 2.5 cm / 1 inch cubes
salt and pepper
60 ml / 4 tbsp oil
1 large onion, chopped
4 celery sticks, sliced
1 green pepper, seeded and chopped
2 garlic cloves, crushed
1 large potato, cut into 2.5 cm / 1 inch cubes
1 large carrot, diced
5–10 ml / 1–2 tsp chilli powder
15 ml / 1 tbsp ground coriander
15 ml / 1 tbsp ground cumin
100 g / 4 oz mushrooms, sliced
2 (397 g / 14 oz) cans chopped tomatoes
2 (425 g / 15 oz) cans red kidney beans, drained
2 courgettes, halved lengthways and cut into chunks
100 g / 4 oz frozen cut green beans or peas

Place the aubergine cubes in a colander, sprinkling thoroughly with salt. Leave for 30 minutes. Rinse and dry the cubes on absorbent kitchen paper.

Heat the oil and fry the onion, celery, pepper and garlic until the onion is slightly softened. Stir in the aubergine and cook, stirring, until the outside of the cubes are lightly cooked. Stir in the potato, carrot, chilli, coriander and cumin. Stir for a few minutes to coat all the vegetables in the spices, then lightly mix in the mushrooms and tomatoes. Bring to the boil, lower the heat so that the mixture simmers and cover. Cook, stirring occasionally, for 30 minutes.

Add the kidney beans, courgettes, beans or peas, with salt and pepper to taste. Cover and continue to cook for a further 30 minutes, stirring occasionally, or until all the vegetables are tender. The juice from the vegetables, combined with the canned tomatoes, should be sufficient to keep the mixture moist. If the mixture cooks too quickly the liquid will evaporate and the vegetables may stick to the pan.

SERVES FOUR

Salads

*Crisp and refreshing or full-flavoured
and satisfying, salads play many roles
in the modern menu. Green salads highlight
rich main courses, whereas protein-based
salads provide delicious lunch dishes
when accompanied by crusty bread.*

FOR AN EXCELLENT SALAD

- Ingredients both raw and cooked must be fresh and in prime condition.
- Select ingredients which complement each other in flavour and texture.
- Do not use so many ingredients that the salad ends up as a kaleidoscope of unrecognizable, clashing flavours.
- Ingredients such as cut beetroot, which discolour or shed colour, should be prepared and added just before serving.
- Salads, salad leaves and greens which become limp quickly should be dressed at the last minute.
- The salad dressing should moisten, blend and develop the flavour of the main ingredients. It should not dominate the dish in any way.

SIDE SALADS

Choose ingredients and a dressing which complement the main food. Side salads should be simple, with clearly defined flavours and a light dressing.

- **Plain Green Salad** Do not underestimate the value of a good, crisp, really fresh lettuce lightly tossed with a well-seasoned, oil-based dressing. This makes an ideal accompaniment for grilled fish, meat or poultry, or may be served with the cheese course. A classic green salad accentuates the richness of the main dish and refreshes the palate.
- **Mixed Green Salad** This should consist of green ingredients, for example salad leaves, cucumber, green pepper, celery, spring onions, watercress, mustard and cress, and avocado. These flavours go together well; a mixed green salad is ideal for serving with foods such as a quiche, with baked potatoes (topped with low-fat soft cheese, butter, soured cream or fromage frais) and with cold roast meats or grilled pork sausages.
- **Mixed Salad** This type of side salad usually consists of a base of leaves, with other green ingredients, topped with raw items, such as tomatoes, radishes and red or yellow peppers. A mixed salad goes well with cold meats and poultry, cheese or eggs. The ingredients should complement the main dish – grated carrots, shredded cabbage and beetroot may replace some of the other basic ingredients.
- **Satisfying Side Salads** Pasta, rice, beans, grains and potatoes all make good salads, and do not have to be mixed with a cornucopia of ingredients. They should be perfectly cooked, then tossed with selected herbs, such as parsley,

mint, basil or tarragon. Additional ingredients should be kept to the minimum: chopped spring onions, diced tomato, and/or chopped olives perhaps. In keeping with the main dish, mayonnaise, yogurt, fromage frais, soured cream or an oil-based mixture may be used to dress the salad.

MAIN COURSE SALADS

Fish and seafood, poultry, meat, game and dairy produce all make excellent salads. Beans and pulses are also suitable. The main food should feature in the same way as for a hot dish, with supporting ingredients and a full-flavoured dressing. It should stand out clearly as the star of the salad, without competition from other ingredients. The salad may be served on a base of shredded lettuce and a garnish of herbs, nuts or croûtons of fried bread may be included to balance the texture where necessary. Main course salads often have very plain accompaniments – chunks of crusty bread (or a baked potato for larger appetites) are usually all that is required.

SALAD NICOISE

salt and pepper
225 g / 8 oz French beans, topped and tailed
2 hard-boiled eggs, cut in quarters
3 small tomatoes, cut in quarters
1 garlic clove, crushed
1 (198 g / 7 oz) can tuna, drained and flaked
50 g / 2 oz black olives
1 large lettuce, separated into leaves
1 (50 g / 2 oz) can anchovy fillets, drained, to garnish

DRESSING
45 ml / 3 tbsp olive oil or a mixture of olive and sunflower oil
salt and pepper
pinch of English mustard powder
pinch of caster sugar
15 ml / 1 tbsp wine vinegar

Bring a small saucepan of salted water to the boil. Add the beans and cook for 5–10 minutes or until just tender. Drain, refresh under cold water and drain again.

Make the dressing by mixing all the ingredients in a screw-topped jar. Close the jar tightly; shake vigorously until well blended.

Put the beans into a large bowl with the eggs, tomatoes, garlic, tuna and most of the olives. Pour over the dressing and toss lightly. Add salt and pepper to taste.

Line a large salad bowl with the lettuce leaves. Pile the tuna mixture into the centre and garnish with the remaining olives and the anchovy fillets. Serve at once.

SERVES FOUR TO SIX

BEAN SALAD WITH TUNA

450 g / 1 lb dry flageolet beans, soaked overnight in water to cover
150 g / 5 oz tomatoes, peeled, seeded and chopped
2 spring onions, finely chopped
1 (198 g / 7 oz) can tuna, drained and flaked

DRESSING
90 ml / 6 tbsp sunflower oil
45 ml / 3 tbsp white wine vinegar
1 garlic clove, crushed
15 ml / 1 tbsp chopped parsley

Drain the beans and put them into a saucepan with fresh cold water to cover. Boil briskly for at least 10 minutes, then lower the heat and simmer for about 1 hour or until tender.

Meanwhile make the dressing by mixing all the ingredients in a screw-topped jar. Close the jar tightly; shake vigorously until well blended.

Drain the beans and put them in a bowl. Add the tomatoes, spring onions and tuna and mix well. Pour the cold dressing over the hot beans and the other ingredients and serve at once on small warmed plates.

SERVES FOUR

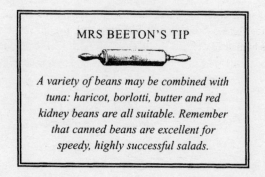

MRS BEETON'S TIP

A variety of beans may be combined with tuna: haricot, borlotti, butter and red kidney beans are all suitable. Remember that canned beans are excellent for speedy, highly successful salads.

CHICKEN AND CELERY SALAD

1 large lettuce, separated into leaves
1 celery heart
350 g / 12 oz cooked chicken, cut into serving pieces
10 ml / 2 tsp tarragon or white wine vinegar
salt and pepper
150 ml / ¼ pint Mayonnaise (page 241)
GARNISH
lettuce leaves
2 hard-boiled eggs, sliced or chopped
stoned black olives and/or gherkin strips

Wash the lettuce leaves and dry them thoroughly. Shred the outer leaves with the celery. Put in a bowl with the chicken and vinegar. Toss lightly and add salt and pepper to taste.

Spoon the chicken mixture into a bowl or on to a platter. Coat with the mayonnaise. Garnish with lettuce leaves, sliced or chopped egg and olives and/or gherkin strips.

SERVES SIX

VARIATION

- If preferred, keep the lettuce heart as a base for the chicken and celery mixture. For a substantial, meal-in-one salad, toss in some cooked pasta shapes or cooked rice.

BEAN SPROUT SALAD

225 g / 8 oz bean sprouts
1 small orange, peeled and sliced
100 g / 4 oz Chinese leaves, shredded
2 celery sticks, thinly sliced
salt and pepper

DRESSING
45 ml / 3 tbsp olive oil or a mixture of olive and sunflower oil
15 ml / 1 tbsp white wine vinegar
1 garlic clove, crushed
2.5 ml / ½ tsp soy sauce
pinch of caster sugar

Pick over the bean sprouts, wash them well, then dry. Cut the orange slices into quarters.

Make the dressing by mixing all the ingredients in a screw-topped jar. Close the jar tightly and shake vigorously.

Combine the bean sprouts, Chinese leaves, celery and orange in a bowl. Pour over the dressing and toss lightly. Season to taste and serve at once.

SERVES FOUR

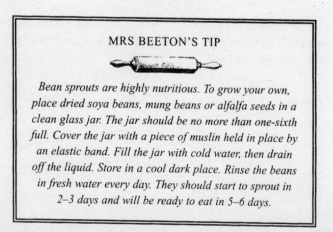

MRS BEETON'S TIP

Bean sprouts are highly nutritious. To grow your own, place dried soya beans, mung beans or alfalfa seeds in a clean glass jar. The jar should be no more than one-sixth full. Cover the jar with a piece of muslin held in place by an elastic band. Fill the jar with cold water, then drain off the liquid. Store in a cool dark place. Rinse the beans in fresh water every day. They should start to sprout in 2–3 days and will be ready to eat in 5–6 days.

COLESLAW

Coleslaw looks marvellous in a natural cabbage bowl. Use a sharp knife to cut out the centre of a Savoy cabbage, using the cut portion for the coleslaw. Rinse the cabbage bowl under cold water, shake off excess moisture and dry between the leaves with absorbent kitchen paper. Trim the base of the cabbage bowl so that it stands neatly.

450 g / 1 lb firm white or Savoy cabbage, finely shredded
100 g / 4 oz carrots, coarsely grated
2 celery sticks, thinly sliced
½ small green pepper, seeded and thinly sliced
150 ml / ¼ pint Mayonnaise (page 241) or plain yogurt
salt and pepper
fresh lemon juice (see method)

Mix all the ingredients in a salad bowl, adding enough lemon juice to give the mayonnaise or yogurt a tangy taste. Chill before serving.

SERVES FOUR

VARIATION

• **Fruit and Nut Slaw** Core and dice, but do not peel, 1 red-skinned eating apple. Toss in 15 ml / 1 tbsp lemon juice, then add to the slaw with 25 g / 1 oz seedless raisins or sultanas and 25 g / 1 oz chopped walnuts, almonds or hazelnuts.

GRAPEFRUIT AND CHICORY SALAD

3 grapefruit
3 small heads of chicory
50 g / 2 oz seedless raisins
15 ml / 1 tbsp grapefruit juice
45 ml / 3 tbsp oil
2.5 ml / ½ tsp French mustard
salt and pepper
mustard and cress to garnish

Cut the grapefruit in half. Cut the fruit into segments and put them into a bowl. Remove all the pulp and pith from the grapefruit shells; stand the shells upside down on absorbent kitchen paper to drain. Shred the chicory, reserving some neat rounds for the garnish, and add to the grapefruit segments with all the remaining ingredients except the garnish. Toss the mixture lightly together, then pile back into the grapefruit shells. Garnish with the cress and reserved chicory and serve at once.

SERVES SIX

CUCUMBER IN YOGURT

1 large cucumber
salt and pepper
300 ml / ½ pint plain or Greek strained yogurt, chilled
15 ml / 1 tsp vinegar (optional)
30 ml / 2 tbsp chopped mint
pinch of sugar

Cut the cucumber into small dice and place it in a colander. Sprinkle with salt, leave for 3–4 hours, then rinse and drain thoroughly. Pat the cucumber dry on absorbent kitchen paper.

Stir the yogurt, vinegar (if used), mint and sugar together in a bowl. Add the cucumber and mix well. Taste and add salt and pepper if required.

SERVES FOUR TO SIX

VARIATION

- **Tzatziki** The combination of cucumber and yogurt is an internationally popular one. This is a Greek-style variation. Grate the cucumber instead of dicing it. Omit the vinegar. The mint is optional but a crushed garlic clove and 15 ml / 1 tbsp finely chopped onion are essential. Mix all the ingredients and serve with warm, fresh bread for a refreshing first course.

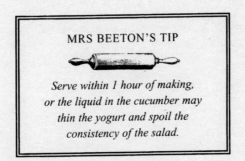

MRS BEETON'S TIP

Serve within 1 hour of making,
or the liquid in the cucumber may
thin the yogurt and spoil the
consistency of the salad.

CAESAR SALAD

*As the egg in this salad is only lightly cooked, it is very important
that it be perfectly fresh, and purchased from a reputable source.*

**3 garlic cloves, peeled but left whole
2 cos lettuces, separated into leaves
150 ml / ¼ pint olive oil
4 large thick slices of bread, crusts removed and cubed
1 egg
juice of 1 lemon
1 (50 g / 2 oz) can anchovy fillets, drained
50 g / 2 oz Parmesan cheese, grated
salt and pepper**

Cut 1 garlic clove in half and rub it all around a salad bowl. Wash the lettuce
leaves and dry them thoroughly. Tear into small pieces and put in the salad bowl.

Heat 60 ml / 4 tbsp of the olive oil in a small frying pan, add the remaining
garlic cloves and fry over gentle heat for 1 minute. Add the bread cubes and fry
until golden on all sides. Remove from the pan with a slotted spoon and drain
on absorbent kitchen paper. Discard the garlic and oil in the pan.

Add the remaining olive oil to the lettuce and toss until every leaf is coated.
Bring a small saucepan of water to the boil, add the egg and cook for 1 minute.
Using a slotted spoon remove it from the water and break it over the lettuce.
Add the lemon juice, anchovies, cheese, salt and pepper and toss lightly.

Add the croûtons of fried bread and toss again. Serve as soon as possible, while
the croûtons are still crisp.

SERVES SIX

RICE SALAD

200 g / 7 oz long-grain rice
salt
60 ml / 4 tbsp olive oil
30 ml / 2 tbsp white wine vinegar
2 spring onions, finely chopped
1 carrot, finely diced and blanched
1 small green pepper, seeded and finely diced
2 gherkins, finely diced
30 ml / 2 tbsp snipped chives
watercress to serve

Place the rice in a saucepan. Pour in 450 ml / ¾ pint cold water. Add a little salt, then bring to the boil. Cover the pan tightly and reduce the heat to the lowest setting. Leave the rice for 15 minutes, turn off the heat and leave for a further 15 minutes without removing the lid. The rice should have absorbed all the liquid. Drain if necessary.

Stir in the oil and vinegar while the rice is still hot. Add the vegetables and chives; mix well. Pile on a dish and garnish with watercress. Serve at once.

SERVES FOUR TO SIX

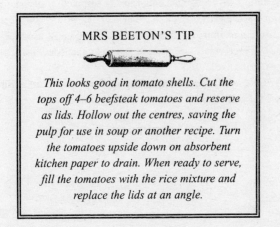

MRS BEETON'S TIP

This looks good in tomato shells. Cut the tops off 4–6 beefsteak tomatoes and reserve as lids. Hollow out the centres, saving the pulp for use in soup or another recipe. Turn the tomatoes upside down on absorbent kitchen paper to drain. When ready to serve, fill the tomatoes with the rice mixture and replace the lids at an angle.

POTATO SALAD

salt and pepper
6 large new potatoes or waxy old potatoes
150 ml / ¼ pint Mayonnaise (page 241)
3 spring onions, chopped
30 ml / 2 tbsp chopped parsley

Bring a saucepan of salted water to the boil, add the potatoes in their jackets and cook for 20–30 minutes until tender. Drain thoroughly. When cool enough to handle, peel and dice the potatoes. Put them in a bowl and add the mayonnaise while still warm. Lightly stir in the spring onions and parsley, with salt and pepper to taste. Cover, leave to become quite cold and stir before serving.

SERVES SIX

VARIATIONS

- **French Potato Salad** Substitute 100 ml / 3½ fl oz French dressing for the mayonnaise. Omit the spring onions, increase the parsley to 45 ml / 3 tbsp and add 5 ml / 1 tsp chopped fresh mint and 5 ml / 1 tsp snipped chives.
- **German Potato Salad** Omit the mayonnaise and spring onions. Reduce the parsley to 5 ml / 1 tsp and add 5 ml / 1 tsp finely chopped onion. Heat 60 ml / 4 tbsp vegetable stock in a saucepan. Beat in 15 ml / 1 tbsp white wine vinegar and 30 ml / 2 tbsp oil. Add salt and pepper to taste. Pour over the diced potatoes while still hot and toss lightly together. Serve at once, or leave to become quite cold.
- **Potato Salad with Apple and Celery** Follow the basic recipe above, but add 2 sliced celery sticks and 1 diced red-skinned apple tossed in a little lemon juice.

MRS BEETON'S POTATO SALAD

*This should be made two or three hours before it is to be served
so that the flavours have time to mature. Cold beef turkey or other
poultry may be thinly sliced or cut into chunks and combined
with the potato salad to make a light main course dish.*

**10 small cold cooked potatoes
60 ml / 4 tbsp tarragon vinegar
90 ml / 6 tbsp salad oil
salt and pepper
15 ml / 1 tbsp chopped parsley**

Cut the potatoes into 1 cm / ½ inch thick slices. For the dressing, mix the
tarragon vinegar, oil and plenty of salt and pepper in a screw-topped jar. Close
the jar tightly and shake vigorously until well blended.

Layer the potatoes in a salad bowl, sprinkling with a little dressing and the
parsley. Pour over any remaining dressing, cover and set aside to marinate
before serving.

SERVES SIX

VARIATIONS

- **Potato and Anchovy Salad** Drain a 50 g / 2 oz can of anchovy fillets,
  reserving the oil. Chop the fillets. Use the oil to make the dressing. Sprinkle
  the chopped anchovies between the layers of potato with the dressing.
- **Potato and Olive Salad** Thinly slice 50 g / 2 oz stoned black olives. Chop
  2 spring onions, if liked, and mix them with the olives. Sprinkle the olives
  between the potato layers.
- **Potato Salad with Pickles** Dice 1 pickled gherkin and 1–2 pickled onions.
  Reduce the vinegar to 15–30 ml / 1–2 tbsp when making the dressing.
  Sprinkle the pickles between the layers of potato with the dressing.

SPINACH AND BACON SALAD

450 g / 1 lb fresh young spinach
150 g / 5 oz button mushrooms, thinly sliced
1 small onion, thinly sliced
15 ml / 1 tbsp oil
6 rindless streaky bacon rashers, cut into strips
75 ml / 5 tbsp French dressing (page 226)

Remove the stalks from the spinach, wash the leaves well in cold water, then dry thoroughly on absorbent kitchen paper. If time permits, put the leaves in a polythene bag and chill for 1 hour.

Tear the spinach into large pieces and put into a salad bowl with the mushrooms and onion.

Heat the oil in a small frying pan and fry the bacon until crisp. Meanwhile toss the salad vegetables with the French dressing. Pour in the hot bacon and fat, toss lightly to mix and serve at once.

SERVES FOUR

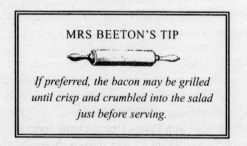

MRS BEETON'S TIP

If preferred, the bacon may be grilled until crisp and crumbled into the salad just before serving.

TOMATO SALAD

Sun-warmed tomatoes, freshly picked, are perfect for this salad.
In the classic Italian version, olive oil is the only dressing,
but a little red wine vinegar may be added, if preferred.

450 g / 1 lb firm tomatoes, peeled and sliced
salt and pepper
pinch of caster sugar (optional)
45 ml / 3 tbsp olive oil
5 ml / 1 tsp chopped fresh basil
fresh basil sprigs to garnish

Put the tomatoes in a serving dish and sprinkle lightly with salt and pepper. Add the sugar, if used. Pour over the olive oil and sprinkle with chopped basil. Garnish with basil sprigs.

SERVES FOUR TO SIX

VARIATIONS

- **Mozzarella and Tomato Salad** Interleave the sliced tomatoes with sliced mozzarella cheese. Cover and leave to marinate for at least an hour before serving.
- **Tomato and Onion Salad** A popular salad to serve with cold meats. Omit the basil. Thinly slice 1 red or white onion and separate the slices into rings. Sprinkle these over the tomatoes. Sprinkle with sugar, salt and pepper, and a few drops of cider vinegar as well as the oil.
- **Minted Tomato Salad with Chives** Omit the basil. Sprinkle 15 ml / 1 tbsp chopped fresh mint and 45 ml / 3 tbsp snipped chives over the tomatoes before adding the oil. Garnish with sprigs of mint.

WALDORF SALAD

4 sharp red dessert apples
2 celery sticks, thinly sliced
25 g / 1 oz chopped or broken walnuts
75 ml / 5 tbsp Mayonnaise (page 241)
30 ml / 2 tbsp lemon juice
pinch of salt
lettuce leaves (optional)

Core the apples, but do not peel them. Cut them into dice. Put them in a bowl with the celery and walnuts. Mix the mayonnaise with the lemon juice. Add salt to taste and fold into the apple mixture. Chill. Serve on a bed of lettuce leaves, if liked.

SERVES FOUR

VARIATION

- **Waldorf Salad with Chicken** Make as above, but use only 2 apples. Add 350 g / 12 oz diced cold cooked chicken. For extra flavour and colour, add 50 g / 2 oz small seedless green grapes.

TABBOULEH

This delicious salad is served all over the middle East.
Its central ingredient is bulgur or cracked wheat, which has
been hulled and parboiled. It therefore needs little or no cooking.

125 g / 4½ oz bulgur wheat
2 tomatoes, peeled, seeded and diced
1 small onion, finely chopped
2 spring onions, finely chopped
50 g / 2 oz parsley, very finely chopped
45 ml / 3 tbsp lemon juice
30 ml / 2 tbsp olive oil
salt and pepper
crisp lettuce leaves to serve

Put the bulgur wheat in a large bowl, add water to cover generously and set aside for 45–60 minutes. Line a sieve or colander with a clean tea-towel and strain the bulgur. When most of the liquid has dripped through, scoop the bulgur up in the tea-towel and squeeze it strongly to extract as much of the remaining liquid as possible. Tip the bulgur into a bowl.

Add the tomatoes, onion, spring onions, parsley, lemon juice and oil, with salt and pepper to taste. Mix well.

Dome the tabbouleh in the centre of a large platter. Arrange the lettuce leaves around the rim to be used as scoops.

SERVES SIX TO EIGHT

VARIATION

- **Tabbouleh in Peppers or Tomatoes** Serve tabbouleh in halved, boiled and well-drained pepper shells or in scooped-out tomato shells.

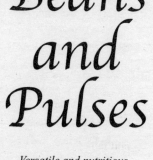

Beans
and
Pulses

*Versatile and nutritious,
beans and pulses are wonderful
for carrying strong flavours.*

COOKING BEANS AND PULSES

The majority of dried beans and pulses should be soaked for several hours or overnight before cooking. Lentils and many brands of dried peas do not require soaking before cooking; however, the following notes apply to other pulses.

- Rinse the pulses, then leave them in plenty of cold water to soak, preferably in a cool place and never for longer than 24 hours.

- Drain, then transfer to a large saucepan and cover with fresh cold water.

- Do not add salt – this toughens the pulses if added before they are thoroughly tender, and they cannot be tenderized once seasoned.

- Bring to the boil and boil rapidly for 10 minutes. This is important as it destroys natural toxins in the pulses.

- Lower the heat, cover and keep the water just boiling.

- The cooking time varies but is usually between 40–60 minutes. Some pulses take longer, up to 1½ hours, and soya beans take 2½ hours or slightly longer.

- Make sure the pulses are covered with water all the time they cook. Drain when tender and use as required.

- When pulses are parboiled, then added to a stew to finish cooking, the stew must not be highly salted or the pulses will toughen.

- Pulses may be added to soups for cooking after the initial boiling period.

CURRIED BEANS

200 g / 7 oz dried haricot beans, soaked overnight in water to cover
30 ml / 2 tbsp oil
1 onion, finely chopped
2.5 cm / 1 inch fresh root ginger, peeled and finely chopped
2 garlic cloves, crushed
pinch of cayenne pepper
15 ml / 1 tbsp ground coriander
2.5 ml / ½ tsp turmeric
30 ml / 2 tbsp brown sugar
1 (397 g / 14 oz) can chopped tomatoes
1 bay leaf
salt and pepper
50 g / 2 oz raisins
1 eating apple, peeled, cored and diced

Drain the beans, put them in a clean saucepan and add fresh water to cover. Bring the water to the boil, boil briskly for 10 minutes, then lower the heat and simmer the beans for about 40 minutes or until just tender.

Meanwhile heat the oil in a large saucepan. Fry the onion, ginger and garlic over gentle heat for about 10 minutes. Stir in cayenne to taste, with the coriander, turmeric and sugar. Fry for 5 minutes more, stirring constantly.

Drain the beans and add them, with the canned tomatoes and bay leaf, to the onion mixture. Add salt and pepper to taste and stir well. Bring just to the boil, then lower the heat and simmer for 30 minutes. Add the raisins and apple, recover and cook gently for a further 30 minutes.

SERVES FOUR

SPICED LENTILS

450 g / 1 lb red lentils
2.5 ml / 1 tsp sea salt
45 ml / 3 tbsp oil
1 onion, chopped
1 small cooking apple, chopped
1.25 ml / ¼ tsp turmeric
1.25 ml / ¼ tsp ground ginger
5 ml / 1 tsp garam masala
5 ml / 1 tsp ground cumin
3 tomatoes, peeled and chopped

GARNISH
chopped fresh coriander leaves
chopped onion or fried onion rings

Put the lentils in a large saucepan with 900 ml / 1½ pints water. Bring to the boil, lower the heat and cover the pan. Simmer gently for 20 minutes. Add the sea salt and simmer for 5 minutes more or until the lentils are soft and all the water has been absorbed.

Meanwhile, heat the oil in a large deep frying pan and add the onion, apple and spices. Fry gently for about 10 minutes until the vegetables are soft and lightly browned. Stir the tomatoes into the pan and cook for 5 minutes, then pour in the lentils.

Stir thoroughly and serve very hot, sprinkled with coriander leaves and onion.

SERVES FOUR TO SIX

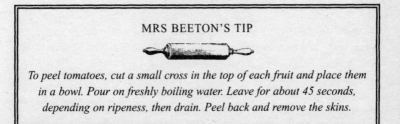

MRS BEETON'S TIP

To peel tomatoes, cut a small cross in the top of each fruit and place them in a bowl. Pour on freshly boiling water. Leave for about 45 seconds, depending on ripeness, then drain. Peel back and remove the skins.

FELAFEL

*Serve felafel in pitta pockets, or omit the tahini and serve
with Greek yogurt and salad for a simple and satisfying lunch.*

200 g / 7 oz chick-peas, soaked overnight
or for several hours in water to cover
75 g / 3 oz fine matzo meal or wholemeal flour
5 ml / 1 tsp salt
5 ml / 1 tsp ground cumin
10 ml / 2 tsp ground coriander
1 garlic clove, crushed
oil for deep frying

TAHINI
50 g / 2 oz ground sesame seeds
1 garlic clove, crushed
1.25 ml / ¼ tsp salt
15 ml / 1 tbsp lemon juice
pinch of pepper

Drain the chick-peas, put them in a clean saucepan and add fresh water to cover. Bring to the boil, lower the heat and simmer for 1–1½ hours until very tender. Drain, mince the chick-peas finely or chop and sieve them.

Combine the minced chick-peas, matzo meal, salt, cumin, coriander and garlic in a bowl. Form into small balls, adding 15–30 ml / 1–2 tbsp water if necessary.

Heat the oil to 170°C / 338°F or until a cube of bread added to the oil browns in 1½ minutes. Add the felafel, a few at a time, and fry until golden brown. Drain on absorbent kitchen paper and keep the felafel hot.

To make the tahini, mix all the ingredients together and add 75 ml / 5 tbsp water. Sieve to a smooth purée or process in a blender or food processor for a few minutes. Add more salt and pepper if required.

MAKES 36

HUMMUS

Serve as a starter or snack, with French bread, pitta or crispbreads.

150 g / 5 oz chick-peas
1 garlic clove, chopped
salt
90 ml / 6 tbsp olive oil
60 ml / 4 tbsp Tahini (bought or see recipe, left)
60 ml / 4 tbsp lemon juice
chopped parsley to garnish

Soak and cook the chick-peas, following the method given for Felafel. Drain thoroughly, then mash and sieve or crush in a mortar with a pestle to a smooth paste. An alternative, and much easier method, is to process the chick-peas in a blender or food processor.

Add the garlic and salt to taste. Stir briskly until well mixed, then gradually work in the olive oil, as when making mayonnaise. The chick-peas should form a creamy paste. Work in the tahini slowly, adding it a teaspoonful at a time at first. When the mixture is creamy work in lemon juice to taste.

Transfer the hummus to a shallow serving bowl and sprinkle with chopped parsley.

SERVES SIX TO EIGHT

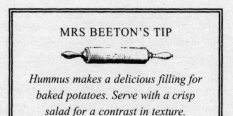

MRS BEETON'S TIP

Hummus makes a delicious filling for baked potatoes. Serve with a crisp salad for a contrast in texture.

HARICOT BEANS WITH ONION AND CARAWAY

200 g / 7 oz haricot beans, soaked overnight in cold water to cover
25 g / 1 oz butter
2 onions, finely chopped
5 ml / 1 tsp caraway seeds
salt and pepper
125 ml / 4 fl oz soured cream
30 ml / 2 tbsp chopped parsley

Drain the beans. Put them in a saucepan with fresh water to cover. Bring to the boil, boil vigorously for 10 minutes, then lower the heat, cover the pan and simmer for about 40 minutes or until the beans are tender. Drain thoroughly.

Melt the butter in a saucepan. Add the onions and caraway seeds and fry for about 10 minutes until just transparent. Add the beans, with salt and pepper to taste, and toss together until heated through.

Spoon into a heated serving dish, top with the soured cream and parsley and serve at once. Alternatively, serve on a bed of red cabbage.

SERVES FOUR TO SIX

MRS BEETON'S TIP

To give the haricot beans extra flavour, cook them in vegetable stock. If you are making your own stock, omit the salt, since this would toughen the beans.

LENTIL PASTIES

100 g / 4 oz split red lentils
300 ml / ½ pint vegetable stock
25 g / 1 oz butter
salt and pepper
pinch of grated nutmeg
4 button mushrooms, sliced
15 ml / 1 tbsp double cream
beaten egg or milk for glazing

SHORT CRUST PASTRY
225 g / 8 oz plain flour
2.5 ml / ½ tsp salt
100 g / 4 oz margarine
flour for rolling out

Make the pastry. Sift the flour and salt into a bowl, then rub in the margarine until the mixture resembles fine breadcrumbs. Add enough cold water to make a stiff dough. Press the dough together with your fingertips. Wrap in grease-proof paper and chill until required.

Put the lentils in a saucepan with the vegetable stock. Bring to the boil, lower the heat and cover the pan. Simmer for 20 minutes or until the lentils are soft and all the liquid is absorbed. Beat in the butter and season with salt, pepper and nutmeg. Stir in the mushrooms and cream. Set aside. Set the oven at 200°C / 400°F / gas 6.

Roll out the pastry very thinly on a floured surface, and cut into eight 13 cm / 5 inch rounds. Divide the lentil filling between the rounds, dampen the edges and fold over to form ½ circles. Press the edges together and seal firmly, then brush with a little beaten egg or milk. Place on baking sheets and bake for about 15 minutes, or until the pastry is cooked and browned.

MAKES EIGHT

LENTIL AND STILTON LASAGNE

*This makes a delicious vegetarian main course which is
full-flavoured and usually enjoyed by non-vegetarians as well.
Serve with a crisp, simple green salad.*

225 g / 8 oz green lentils
8 sheets of lasagne
salt and pepper
30 ml / 2 tbsp olive oil
1 large onion, chopped
1 garlic clove, crushed
5 ml / 1 tsp dried marjoram
225 g / 8 oz mushrooms, sliced
2 (397 g / 14 oz) cans chopped tomatoes
225 g / 8 oz ripe blue Stilton cheese (without rind)
30 ml / 2 tbsp plain flour
300 ml / ½ pint milk

Cook the lentils in plenty of boiling water for 35 minutes, until just tender.
Cook the lasagne in boiling salted water with a little oil added for 12–15
minutes, or until just tender. Drain both and set the lentils aside; lay the lasagne
out to dry on absorbent kitchen paper.

Heat the remaining oil in a large saucepan. Add the onion, garlic and marjoram,
and cook for 10 minutes, or until slightly softened. Stir in the mushrooms and
cook for 5 minutes before adding the tomatoes. Stir in the cooked lentils with
plenty of salt and pepper and bring to the boil. Reduce the heat and cover the
pan, then simmer for 5 minutes.

Set the oven at 180°C / 350°F / gas 4. Grease a lasagne dish or large ovenproof
dish. Pour half the lentil mixture into the base of the dish and top it with half
the lasagne. Pour the remaining lentil mixture over the pasta, then end with the
remaining pasta.

Mash the Stilton in a bowl with a sturdy fork or process it in a food processor.
Sprinkle a little of the flour over the cheese and work it in, then add the remaining flour in the same way to make the mixture crumbly. Gradually work in the

milk, a little at a time, pounding the cheese at first, then beating it as it softens. When the mixture is soft and creamy, the remaining milk may be incorporated more quickly. Add some pepper and just a little salt. Pour the mixture over the lasagne, scraping the bowl clean. Bake for 40–45 minutes, or until the top of the lasagne is well browned and bubbling.

SERVES SIX

VARIATION

- **Lentil and Leek Lasagne** Omit the onion in the main recipe and use 450 g / 1 lb sliced leeks. Cook them with an additional knob of butter until well reduced. Continue as above. Cheddar may be substituted for the Stilton: it should be finely grated or chopped in a food processor.

THREE-BEAN SAUTE

A quick and easy dish for a light meal, this sauté tastes delicious
when served on a base of mixed green salad – crunchy Iceberg lettuce,
some thinly sliced green pepper and sliced cucumber.

100 g / 4 oz shelled broad beans
juice of 2 oranges
2 carrots, cut into matchstick strips
225 g / 8 oz fine French beans
salt and pepper
30 ml / 2 tbsp oil
1 onion, halved and thinly sliced
2 (425 g / 15 oz) cans butter beans, drained
30 ml / 2 tbsp chopped parsley
4 tomatoes, peeled, seeded and cut into eighths

Place the broad beans in a saucepan with the orange juice. Add just enough water to cover the beans, then bring to the boil. Lower the heat slightly so that the beans simmer steadily. Cook for 5 minutes.

Add the carrots and French beans, mix well and sprinkle in a little salt and pepper. Continue to cook, stirring often, until the carrots are just tender and the liquid has evaporated to leave the vegetables juicy. Set aside.

Heat the oil in a clean saucepan and cook the onion until softened but not browned – about 10 minutes. Stir in the butter beans and parsley, and cook for 5 minutes, stirring until the beans are hot. Tip the carrot mixture into the pan, add the tomatoes and mix well. Cook for 1–2 minutes before serving.

SERVES FOUR

SPICY SPINACH AND CHICK-PEAS

The use of canned chick-peas makes this delicious dish a quick-cook option.

25 g / 1 oz butter
30 ml / 2 tbsp cumin seeds
15 ml / 1 tbsp coriander seeds, crushed
15 ml / 1 tbsp mustard seeds
1 large onion, chopped
2 garlic cloves, crushed
2 (425 g / 15 oz) cans chick-peas, drained
5 ml / 1 tsp turmeric
1 kg / 2¼ lb fresh spinach, cooked
salt and pepper

Melt the butter in a saucepan, add the cumin, coriander and mustard seeds and cook gently, stirring, for about 3 minutes, or until the seeds are aromatic. Keep the heat low to avoid burning the butter.

Add the onion and garlic to the pan and continue to cook for about 15 minutes, until the onion is softened. Stir in the chick-peas and turmeric and cook for 5 minutes, until thoroughly hot. Tip the spinach into the pan and stir it over moderate heat until heated through. Season and serve.

SERVES FOUR TO SIX

TOFU AND SPRING ONION STIR FRY

This tasty stir fry goes well with cooked rice or Oriental noodles.

350 g / 12 oz firm tofu cut into 2.5 cm / 1 inch cubes
1 garlic clove, crushed
45 ml / 3 tbsp soy sauce
5 cm / 2 inch fresh root ginger, peeled and chopped
5 ml / 1 tsp sesame oil
5 ml / 1 tsp cornflour
30 ml / 2 tbsp dry sherry
60 ml / 4 tbsp vegetable stock
30 ml / 2 tbsp oil
1 red pepper, seeded and diced
1 bunch of spring onions, trimmed and sliced diagonally
100 g / 4 oz button mushrooms, sliced
salt and pepper

Place the tofu in a large, shallow dish. Mix the garlic, soy sauce, ginger and sesame oil in a bowl, then sprinkle the mixture evenly over the tofu. Cover and leave to marinate for 1 hour. In a jug, blend the cornflour to a paste with the sherry, then stir in the stock and set aside.

Heat the oil in a wok or large frying pan. Add the tofu and stir fry until lightly browned. Add the pepper and continue cooking for 2–3 minutes before stirring in the spring onions. Once the onions are combined with the tofu, make a space in the middle of the pan and stir fry the mushrooms for 2 minutes. Pour in the cornflour mixture and stir all the ingredients together. Bring the juices to the boil, stirring all the time, then lower the heat and simmer for 2 minutes. Taste the mixture for seasoning, then serve.

SERVES FOUR

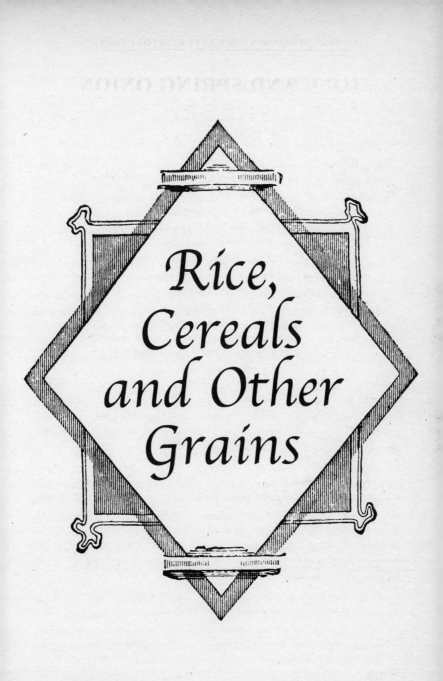

Rice, Cereals and Other Grains

COOKING RICE

225 g / 8 oz long-grain rice
salt and pepper

If using Basmati rice, plain, untreated long-grain rice or wild rice, start by placing the grains in a bowl. Wash the rice in several changes of cold water, taking care not to swirl the grains vigorously as this may damage them. Pour off most of the water each time, then add fresh water and swirl the rice gently with your fingertips. Finally drain the rice in a sieve and turn it into a saucepan.

Add cold water: 600 ml / 1 pint for white rice; 750 ml / 1¼ pints for brown or wild rice. Add a little salt and bring to the boil. Stir once, then lower the heat and put a tight-fitting lid on the pan. Cook very gently until the grains are tender: 15–20 minutes for easy-cook varieties and white rice; 20 minutes for Basmati rice; 25–35 minutes for brown rice; 40–50 minutes for wild rice.

Remove the pan from the heat and leave, covered, for 5 minutes, then fork up the grains, add salt and pepper if liked, and serve the rice.

SERVES FOUR

VARIATIONS

- **Saffron Rice** Add 3 green cardamom pods and a bay leaf to the rice. Reduce the amount of water by 50 ml / 2 fl oz. Pound 2.5–5 ml / ½–1 tsp saffron strands to a powder in a mortar with a pestle. Add 50 ml / 2 fl oz boiling water and stir well until the saffron has dissolved. Sprinkle this over the rice after it has been cooking for 15 minutes, then replace the lid quickly and finish cooking. Fork up the rice before serving, removing the bay leaf and cardamoms.
- **Pilau Rice** Cook 1 chopped onion in a little butter or ghee in a large saucepan, then add 1 cinnamon stick, 1 bay leaf, 4 green cardamoms and 4 cloves. Stir in 225 g / 8 oz Basmati rice and 600 ml / 1 pint water and cook as in the main recipe. In a separate pan, cook a second onion, this time thinly sliced, in 50 g / 2 oz butter or ghee until golden brown. Add 30 ml / 2 tbsp cumin seeds (preferably black seeds) when the onion has softened and

before it begins to brown. Add half the sliced onion mixture to the rice and fork it in. Pour the remaining onion mixture over the top of the rice before serving. Saffron may be added to pilau.

- **Brown and Wild Rice** Mix different grains for an interesting texture. Start by cooking the wild rice for 10 minutes, then add the brown rice and continue cooking until the brown rice is tender.
- **Lemon Rice** Add the grated rind of 1 lemon to the rice: if it is added at the beginning of cooking it gives a deep-seated flavour; added just before serving it adds a fresh, zesty tang to the rice.
- **Rice with Herbs** Add bay leaves, sprigs of rosemary, thyme, savory or sage to the rice at the beginning of cooking. Alternatively, sprinkle chopped parsley, fresh tarragon, dill, mint or marjoram over the rice at the end of cooking. Match the herb to the flavouring in the main dish, with which the rice is to be served.

PAELLA VALENCIANA

1 kg / 2¼ lb mussels, washed, scraped and bearded
30 ml / 2 tbsp plain flour
1 (1. 5 kg / 3¼ lb) roasting chicken, cut into portions
90 ml / 6 tbsp olive oil
2 garlic cloves
675g / 1½ lb risotto rice
pinch of saffron threads
salt

GARNISH
450 g / 1 lb cooked shellfish
(prawns, crayfish, lobster or crab; see Mrs Beeton's Tip)
strips of canned pimiento green or black olives
chopped parsley

Wash, scrape and beard the mussels. Put them in a large saucepan with 125 ml / 4 fl oz water. Place over moderate heat and bring to the boil. As soon as the liquid bubbles up over the mussels, shake the pan two or three times, cover, lower the heat and simmer until the mussels have opened. Discard any that remain shut. Remove the mussels with a slotted spoon and shell them, retaining the best half shells. Strain the mussel liquid through muslin into a large measuring jug, add the cooking liquid and make up to 1.25 litres / 2¼ pints with water. Set aside.

Put the flour in a stout polythene bag, add the chicken portions and shake until well coated. Heat 45 ml / 3 tbsp of the olive oil in a large frying pan, add the chicken and fry until golden brown on all sides. Using tongs, transfer the chicken to a plate and set aside.

Heat the remaining oil in a large deep frying pan or paella pan. Slice half a garlic clove thinly and add the slices to the oil. Fry until golden brown, then discard the garlic. Add the rice to the pan and fry very gently, turning frequently with a spatula. Crush the remaining garlic. Pound the saffron to a powder with a pestle in a mortar and sprinkle it over the rice with the garlic. Add salt to taste.

Add the reserved cooking liquid to the pan and heat to simmering point, stirring frequently. Cook for 5 minutes, still stirring. Add the chicken pieces, cooking them with the rice for 15–20 minutes until they are tender and the rice is cooked through.

Garnish with the shellfish, pimiento olives and parsley. Replace the mussels in the half shells and arrange them on top of the rice mixture. Remove the pan from the heat, cover with a clean cloth and set aside for 10 minutes before serving. Serve from the pan.

SERVES EIGHT

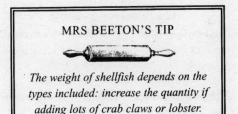

MRS BEETON'S TIP

The weight of shellfish depends on the types included: increase the quantity if adding lots of crab claws or lobster.

KOULIBIAC

Koulibiac is a large oblong pastry filled with a mixture of cooked rice and salmon. Smoked salmon offcuts or canned salmon may be used instead of fresh salmon. Instead of following the method described below, cook the fish on a covered plate which fits tightly over the saucepan, if preferred. This is good either hot or cold and is therefore ideal for formal meals, buffets or picnics.

fat for greasing
450 g / 1 lb salmon fillet or stealks
salt and pepper
juice of ½ lemon
175 g / 6 oz long-grain rice
50 g / 2 oz butter
1 onion, chopped
60 ml / 4 tbsp chopped parsley
4 hard-boiled eggs, roughly chopped
15 ml / 1 tbsp chopped fresh tarragon (optional)
450 g / 1 lb puff pastry
1 egg, beaten, to glaze
150 ml / ¼ pint soured cream to serve

Lay the salmon on a piece of greased foil large enough to enclose it completely. Sprinkle with salt, pepper and a little of the lemon juice, then wrap the foil around the fish, sealing the edges.

Place the rice in a large saucepan and add 450 ml / ¾ pint water. Bring to the boil, lower the heat and cover the pan. Simmer the rice for 10 minutes, then place the foil-wrapped fish on top of the rice. Cover the pan again and cook for about 10 minutes more or until the grains of rice are tender and all the water has been absorbed.

At the end of the cooking time, remove the foil-packed salmon from the pan. Transfer the fish to a board, reserving all the cooking juices, then discard the skin and any bones. Coarsely flake the flesh and set the fish aside. Tip the cooked rice into a bowl.

Melt half the butter in a small saucepan. Add the onion and cook over low heat for about 15 minutes until it is soft but not browned. Mix the cooked onion with the rice and add the salmon and parsley, with salt and pepper to taste. Put the chopped hard-boiled eggs in a bowl. Stir in the remaining lemon juice and add the tarragon, if used. Melt the remaining butter and trickle it over the eggs.

Set the oven at 220°C / 425°F / gas 7. Cut a large sheet of foil, at least 30 cm / 12 inches long. On a floured board, roll out the pastry to a rectangle measuring about 50 x 25 cm / 20 x 10 inches. Trim the pastry to 43 x 25 cm / 17 x 10 inches. Cut the trimmings into long narrow strips. Set aside.

Lay the pastry on the foil. Spoon half the rice mixture lengthways down the middle of the pastry. Top with the egg mixture in an even layer, then mound the remaining mixture over the top. Fold one long side of pastry over the filling and brush the edge with beaten egg. Fold the other side over and press the long edges together firmly. Brush the inside of the pastry at the ends with egg and seal them firmly.

Use the foil to turn the koulibiac over so that the pastry seam is underneath, then lift it on to a baking sheet or roasting tin. Brush all over with beaten egg and arrange the reserved strips of pastry in a lattice pattern over the top. Brush these with egg too.

Bake the koulibiac for 30–40 minutes, until the pastry is well puffed and golden. Check after 25 minutes and if the pastry looks well browned, tent a piece of foil over the top to prevent it from overcooking.

Serve a small dish of soured cream with the koulibiac, which should be cut into thick slices.

SERVES EIGHT

RISOTTO MILANESE

75 g / 3 oz butter
30 ml / 2 tbsp olive oil
1 onion, finely chopped
350 g / 12 oz risotto rice
600 ml / 1 pint vegetable stock
2.5 ml / 1 tsp saffron threads
300 ml / ½ pint dry white wine
salt and pepper
150 g / 5 oz Parmesan cheese, grated

Heat 25 g / 1 oz of the butter with the olive oil in a large saucepan. Add the onion and fry gently, stirring occasionally for 10 minutes. Add the rice and cook for a few minutes, stirring gently until all the rice grains are coated in fat. Meanwhile heat the stock to simmering point in a separate pan.

Put the saffron threads in a mortar and pound them with a pestle. Stir in a little of the hot stock to dissolve the saffron, then set aside.

Add the wine and half the remaining stock to the rice, with salt and pepper to taste. Bring to the boil. Stir once, lower the heat and cover the pan tightly. Leave over low heat for 10 minutes. Pour in half the remaining hot stock, do not stir, then cover and cook for 5 minutes, shaking the pan occasionally to prevent sticking. Finally, add the remaining stock and saffron liquid. Stir once or twice, cover and cook for about 10 minutes, until the rice is cooked, creamy and moist.

Stir in the remaining butter and the cheese. Taste the risotto, adding more salt and pepper if required. Cover tightly and leave to stand for 5 minutes before serving.

SERVES FOUR

KEDGEREE

No Victorian country-house breakfast would
have been complete without kedgeree.

salt and pepper
150 g / 5 oz long-grain rice
125 ml / 4 fl oz milk
450 g / 1 lb smoked haddock
50 g / 2 oz butter
15 ml / 1 tbsp curry powder
2 hard-boiled eggs, roughly chopped
cayenne pepper

GARNISH
15 g / ½ oz butter
1 hard-boiled egg, white and yolk sieved separately
15 ml / 1 tbsp chopped parsley

Bring a saucepan of salted water to the boil. Add the rice and cook for 12 minutes. Drain thoroughly, rinse under cold water and drain again. Place the strainer over a saucepan of simmering water to keep the rice warm.

Put the milk in a large shallow saucepan or frying pan with 125 ml / 4 fl oz water. Bring to simmering point, add the fish and poach gently for 4 minutes. Using a slotted spoon and a fish slice, transfer the haddock to a wooden board.

Remove the skin and any bones from the haddock and break up the flesh into fairly large flakes. Melt half the butter in a large saucepan. Blend in the curry powder and add the flaked fish. Warm the mixture through. Remove from the heat, lightly stir in the chopped eggs; add salt, pepper and cayenne.

Melt the remaining butter in a second pan, add the rice, salt, pepper and cayenne. Add to the haddock and mix well. Pile the kedgeree on to a warmed dish, dot with butter, garnish with sieved hard-boiled egg yolk, egg white and parsley and serve at once.

SERVES FOUR

SCAMPI JAMBALAYA

25 g / 1 oz butter
15 ml / 1 tbsp oil
2 onions, finely chopped
100 g / 4 oz cooked ham, diced
3 tomatoes, peeled and chopped
1 green pepper, seeded and finely chopped
1 garlic clove, crushed
pinch of dried thyme
salt and pepper
cayenne pepper
5 ml / 1 tsp Worcestershire sauce
225 g / 8 oz long-grain rice
125 ml / 4 fl oz hot chicken stock
450 g / 1 lb peeled cooked scampi tails
100 g / 4 oz shelled cooked mussels (optional)
30 ml / 2 tbsp medium-dry sherry
fresh thyme sprigs to garnish

Melt the butter in the oil in a deep frying pan. Add the onions and fry gently for 4–5 minutes until soft. Add the ham, tomatoes, green pepper and garlic, then stir in the thyme, with salt, pepper and cayenne to taste. Add the Worcestershire sauce and rice. Stir well. Pour in the hot chicken stock, cover the pan and cook for 12 minutes.

Add the scampi to the pan, with the mussels, if used. Lower the heat, cover and simmer for 5 minutes more or until the rice is perfectly cooked. Stir in the sherry, garnish with thyme and serve at once.

SERVES FOUR

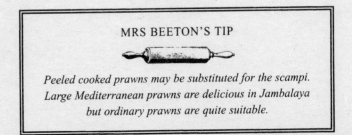

MRS BEETON'S TIP

Peeled cooked prawns may be substituted for the scampi. Large Mediterranean prawns are delicious in Jambalaya but ordinary prawns are quite suitable.

POLENTA WITH SMOKED SAUSAGE

The sausages used in this satisfying dish are dried continental ones.
They have a high meat content and require a little cooking before eating.

400 g / 14 oz polenta
salt and pepper
400 g / 14 oz chorizo, cabanos or other small smoked sausages
200 g / 7 oz tomato purée
50 g / 2 oz Parmesan cheese, grated
25 g / 1 oz dried white breadcrumbs
25 g / 1 oz butter

Bring 500 ml / 17 fl oz water to the boil in a large saucepan. Stir in the polenta and salt and pepper to taste. Cook for 10–15 minutes, stirring all the time. Leave to cool.

Cook the sausages in boiling water for 10 minutes. Remove from the pan and leave to cool. Remove the skins and cut into 2 cm / ¾ inch slices.

Set the oven at 180°C / 350°F / gas 4. Put a layer of polenta in the bottom of an ovenproof dish, cover with a layer of sausages, some tomato purée, Parmesan, salt and pepper. Repeat the layers until all the ingredients have been used. Sprinkle the breadcrumbs over the mixture. Dot with the butter. Bake for 25–30 minutes.

SERVES THREE TO FOUR

SEMOLINA GNOCCHI

Serve this Italian-style dish with a tomato sauce or spicy savoury sauce.
The gnocchi may be cooked in the oven or under the grill.

fat for greasing
500 ml / 17 fl oz milk
100 g / 4 oz semolina
salt and pepper
1.25 ml / ¼ tsp grated nutmeg
1 egg
100 g / 4 oz Parmesan cheese, grated
25 g / 1 oz butter

Grease a shallow ovenproof dish. Bring the milk to the boil in a saucepan. Sprinkle in the semolina and stir over low heat until the mixture is thick. Mix in the salt, pepper, nutmeg, egg and 75 g / 3 oz of the Parmesan. Beat the mixture well until smooth. Spread on a shallow dish and leave to cool.

Set the oven at 200°C / 400°F / gas 6, if using. Cut the cooled semolina mixture into 2 cm / ¾ inch squares or shape into rounds. Place in the prepared ovenproof dish and sprinkle with the remaining Parmesan; dot with butter. Brown under the grill or in the oven for 8–10 minutes.

SERVES FOUR

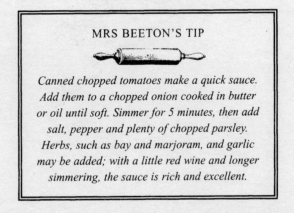

MRS BEETON'S TIP

Canned chopped tomatoes make a quick sauce.
Add them to a chopped onion cooked in butter
or oil until soft. Simmer for 5 minutes, then add
salt, pepper and plenty of chopped parsley.
Herbs, such as bay and marjoram, and garlic
may be added; with a little red wine and longer
simmering, the sauce is rich and excellent.

CORN PUDDING

fat for greasing
100 g / 4 oz plain flour
5 ml / 1 tsp salt
2.5 ml / ½ tsp black pepper
2 eggs, beaten
500 ml / 17 fl oz milk
400 g / 14 oz fresh or frozen sweetcorn kernels

Grease a 1.5 litre / 2¾ pint pie or ovenproof dish. Set the oven at 180°C / 350°F / gas 4. Sift the flour, salt and pepper into a bowl. Add the beaten eggs, stirring well. Beat together with the milk and then the corn to form a batter. Turn into the prepared dish. Bake for 1 hour. Serve.

SERVES SIX

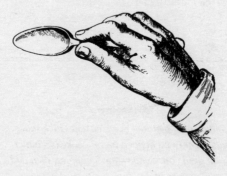

COUSCOUS

50 g / 2 oz chick-peas, soaked overnight in plenty of cold water
45 ml / 3 tbsp olive oil
8 chicken thighs, skinned if preferred
2 garlic cloves, crushed
1 large onion, chopped
1 green pepper, seeded and sliced
1 green chilli, seeded and chopped (optional)
15 ml / 1 tbsp ground coriander
5 ml / 1 tsp ground cumin
100 g / 4 oz carrots, sliced
100 g / 4 oz turnips, cut into chunks
450 g / 1 lb pumpkin, peeled, seeds removed and cut into chunks
450 g / 1 lb potatoes, cut into chunks
1 bay leaf
2 (397 g / 14 oz) cans chopped tomatoes
50 g / 2 oz raisins
150 ml / ¼ pint chicken stock or water
salt and pepper
225 g / 8 oz courgettes, sliced
45 ml / 3 tbsp chopped parsley
350 g / 12 oz couscous
50 g / 2 oz butter, melted

Drain the chick-peas, then cook them in plenty of fresh boiling water for 10 minutes. Lower the heat, cover the pan and simmer for 1½ hours, or until the chick-peas are just tender. Drain.

Heat the oil in a very large flameproof casserole or saucepan. Add the chicken pieces and brown them all over, then use a slotted spoon to remove them from the pan and set aside. Add the garlic, onion, pepper and chilli, if used, to the oil remaining in the pan and cook for 5 minutes, stirring.

Stir in the coriander and cumin, then add the carrots, turnips, pumpkin, potatoes, bay leaf, tomatoes, raisins, stock or water with salt and pepper to taste. Stir in the drained chick-peas. Bring to the boil, then lower the heat and replace the chicken thighs, tucking them in among the vegetables. Cover and simmer

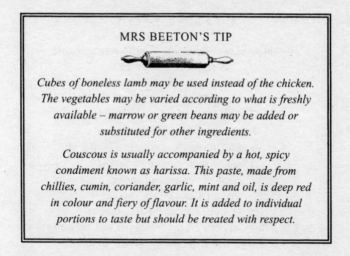

MRS BEETON'S TIP

*Cubes of boneless lamb may be used instead of the chicken.
The vegetables may be varied according to what is freshly
available – marrow or green beans may be added or
substituted for other ingredients.*

*Couscous is usually accompanied by a hot, spicy
condiment known as harissa. This paste, made from
chillies, cumin, coriander, garlic, mint and oil, is deep red
in colour and fiery of flavour. It is added to individual
portions to taste but should be treated with respect.*

gently for 1 hour. Stir in the courgettes and parsley, cover the pan and continue to cook gently for a further 30 minutes.

There are two options for preparing the couscous. The first is to line a steamer with scalded muslin, then sprinkle the couscous into it. Place the steamer over the simmering stew for the final 30 minutes' cooking, covering it tightly to keep all the steam in. Alternatively – and this is the easier method – place the couscous in a deep casserole or bowl and pour in fresh boiling water from the kettle to cover the grains by 2.5 cm / 1 inch. Cover and set aside for 15 minutes. The grains will absorb the boiling water and swell. If the couscous cools on standing, it may be reheated over a pan of boiling water or in a microwave for about 2 minutes on High.

To serve, transfer the couscous to a very large serving dish and pour the hot melted butter over it. Fork up the grains and make a well in the middle. Ladle the chicken and vegetable stew into the well, spooning cooking juices over the couscous.

SERVES EIGHT

Pasta

As versatile as the British potato,
pasta is favoured all over the world.
A deliciously simple way to dress piping hot pasta
is with olive oil, garlic, basil or parsley,
freshly-ground black pepper and
grated Parmesan cheese.

PASTA

Home-made pasta dough may be used to make noodles,
lasagne or stuffed pasta (such as ravioli). Alternatively,
it may be cut into small squares for cooking.

400 g / 14 oz strong white flour
2.5 ml / ½ tsp salt
30 ml / 2 tbsp olive oil or 40 g / 1 ½ oz butter, melted
3 eggs, beaten
about 15 ml / 1 tbsp oil for cooking
about 50 g / 2 oz butter
freshly-ground black pepper

Put the flour and salt in a large bowl and make a well in the middle. Add the oil or butter and the eggs, then gradually mix in the flour to make a stiff dough. As the mixture clumps together use your hands to knead it into one piece. If necessary add 15–30 ml/ 1–2 tbsp water, but take care not to make the mixture soft. It should be quite hard at this stage as it will become more pliable on kneading.

Knead the dough thoroughly on a very lightly floured surface for 10–15 minutes, or until it is very smooth and pliable. Ideally you should be able to work without dusting the surface with flour more than once, provided you keep the dough moving fairly fast all the time.

Cut the dough in half and wrap one piece in polythene to prevent it from drying out. Roll out the dough, adding a dusting of flour as necessary, into a large thin oblong sheet.

To cut noodles, dust the dough with flour and fold it in half, dust it again and fold over once more. Cut the folded dough into 1 cm / ½ inch wide strips, then shake them out and place on a floured plate. Cover loosely with polythene to prevent them from drying out until they are cooked. Repeat with the remaining dough.

Bring a very large saucepan of salted water to the boil. Add a little oil. Tip all the noodles into the pan and bring the water back to the boil rapidly, stir once, then regulate the heat so that the water boils but does not froth over. Cook for about 3 minutes. The pasta should be tender but not soft.

continues overleaf ...

Drain the pasta and turn it into a heated bowl. Toss a knob of butter and plenty of freshly-ground black pepper with the noodles, then serve piping hot.

MAKES ABOUT 450 G / 1 LB

VARIATIONS

- **Pasta Verde** Cook 225 g / 8 oz fresh spinach, or 100 g / 4 oz frozen chopped spinach. Drain the spinach thoroughly and purée in a blender or food processor. When making the pasta, use an extra 50 g / 2 oz plain flour. Add the spinach purée to the well in the flour and mix it in with the eggs. It will not be necessary to add any water.
- **Tomato Pasta** Mix 30 ml / 2 tbsp tomato purée with the oil or butter, then stir in the eggs before incorporating the mixture with the flour.

FREEZER TIP

Roll out and cut up the pasta, then freeze in practical quantities. Fresh pasta cooks from frozen, taking 2–3 minutes longer than usual.

STUFFED BAKED CANNELLONI

butter for greasing
12–16 cannelloni
15 ml / 1 tbsp olive oil
300 g / 11 oz frozen chopped spinach
salt and pepper
1.25 ml / ¼ tsp grated nutmeg
150 g / 5 oz ricotta or cottage cheese
50 g / 2 oz cooked ham, finely chopped
600 ml / 1 pint Cheese Sauce (page 230)
25 g / 1 oz dried white breadcrumbs
25 g / 1 oz Parmesan cheese, grated

Butter an ovenproof dish. Set the oven at 180°C / 350°F / gas 5. Cook the cannelloni in a saucepan of boiling salted water with the oil for 10–15 minutes until tender but still firm to the bite. Drain well.

Place the spinach in a saucepan. Cook over low heat for about 10 minutes or until the spinach has thawed completely. Raise the temperature and heat the spinach thoroughly. Drain. Mix the spinach, salt, pepper, nutmeg, soft cheese and ham in a bowl. Spoon the mixture into the cannelloni. Place in the prepared ovenproof dish. Pour the sauce over the cannelloni.

Bake for 15–20 minutes. Mix together the crumbs and Parmesan, then sprinkle over the dish. Place under a hot grill for 2–3 minutes to brown the top.

SERVES FOUR

SEAFOOD LASAGNE

butter for greasing
12 sheets of lasagne
25 g / 1 oz butter
1 onion, chopped
1 celery stick, diced
25 g / 1 oz plain flour
300 ml / ½ pint red wine
45 ml / 3 tbsp tomato purée
1 bay leaf
60 ml / 4 tbsp chopped parsley
salt and pepper
450 g / 1 lb, white fish fillet, skinned and cut into small pieces
225 g / 8 oz peeled cooked prawns, thawed if frozen
225 g / 8 oz shelled cooked mussels, thawed if frozen
100 g / 4 oz mushrooms, sliced
100 g / 4 oz mozzarella cheese, diced
600 ml / 1 pint White Sauce (page 230)

Grease a large lasagne dish with butter. Cook the lasagne if necessary (if using lasagne which requires no pre-cooking, follow package instructions) and leave to dry.

Melt the butter in a saucepan. Add the onion and celery, then cook, stirring occasionally, for 10 minutes. Stir in the flour, then gradually pour in the wine, stirring all the time. Add 125 ml / 4 fl oz water and bring to the boil, stirring. Stir in the tomato purée, bay leaf and parsley. Lower the heat and simmer for 5 minutes. Taste the sauce; add salt and pepper as required.

Set the oven at 180°C / 350°F / gas 4. Remove the wine sauce from the heat. Add the fish, prawns and mussels. Make sure that any frozen seafood is well drained. Lastly, stir in the mushrooms.

Place a layer of lasagne in the prepared dish, then top with half the seafood sauce. Lay half the remaining lasagne over the sauce, then pour on all the remaining seafood mixture. Top with the rest of the lasagne. Stir the mozzarella into the white sauce, then pour this over the lasagne.

Bake for 20–40 minutes until golden brown and bubbling hot. (The type of pasta used will dictate the exact timing.) If liked, serve with salad and crusty bread to mop up the sauce.

SERVES SIX

SPAGHETTI ALLA CARBONARA

450 g / 1 lb spaghetti salt and pepper
15 ml / 1 tbsp oil
100 g / 4 oz rindless streaky bacon rashers, cut into fine strips
4 eggs
30 ml / 2 tbsp double cream
75 g / 3 oz Pecorino or Parmesan cheese, grated

Cook the spaghetti in a large saucepan of boiling salted water for 8–10 minutes or until tender but still firm to the bite.

Meanwhile heat the oil in a large frying pan and fry the bacon until the fat is transparent. Draw the pan off the heat. In a bowl, beat the eggs with the cream, adding a little salt and a generous grinding of pepper.

Drain the cooked spaghetti thoroughly and mix it with the bacon. Return to moderate heat for 1–2 minutes to heat through. Stir the egg mixture rapidly into the pan. As it begins to thicken, tip in the cheese. Do not stir it in. Serve immediately on hot plates.

SERVES FOUR

LASAGNE AL FORNO

150 g / 5 oz lasagne (7 sheets)
or 200 g / 7 oz (12 sheets) no-precook lasagne
30 ml / 2 tbsp oil
2 onions, finely chopped
2 garlic cloves, chopped
225 g / 8 oz minced beef
225 g / 8 oz minced pork
100 g / 4 oz mushrooms, sliced
2 (397 g / 14 oz) cans chopped tomatoes
2.5 ml / ½ tsp dried basil
2.5 ml / ½ tsp dried oregano
150 ml / ¼ pint red wine
salt and pepper
900 ml / 1½ pints cold White Sauce (page 230)
50 g / 2 oz Parmesan cheese, grated

Cook the lasagne, if necessary, in plenty of boiling salted water. Add the lasagne a sheet at a time, then boil for about 12 minutes until tender but not soft. Drain well, rinse under cold water and lay out to dry on absorbent kitchen paper.

Heat the oil in a heavy-bottomed saucepan, add the onions and garlic and fry over medium heat for 10 minutes. Stir in the beef and pork. Cook, stirring, for 5–10 minutes.

Stir in the mushrooms, tomatoes, herbs and wine. Add salt and pepper. Bring just to the boil, stirring. Reduce the heat, then simmer the sauce steadily, uncovered, stirring occasionally. Allow 1¼–1½ hours until the meat is tender and the sauce thick when stirred.

Set the oven at 180°C / 350°F / gas 4. Spread a thin layer of the white sauce over the base of a 30 x 20 cm / 12 x 8 inch baking dish. Arrange a layer of lasagne in the dish. Top with a layer of meat sauce. Add a thin layer of white sauce, but do not worry too much about spreading the sauce perfectly; the next layer of lasagne will smooth it out. Repeat the layers, ending with white sauce. Sprinkle the top with Parmesan.

Bake for 40–50 minutes, until golden brown. Allow the lasagne to stand for 10 minutes before serving.

SERVES SIX TO EIGHT

CRAB-STUFFED CANNELLONI

fat for greasing
12 cannelloni
salt and pepper
225 g / 8 oz crab meat
50 g / 2 oz fresh white breadcrumbs
3 spring onions, chopped
225 g / 8 oz ricotta cheese
600 ml / 1 pint Fresh Tomato Sauce (page 236)
225 g / 8 oz mozzarella cheese, sliced

Grease a large, shallow baking dish with butter. Alternatively, prepare 4 individual gratin dishes. Cook the cannelloni in boiling salted water for 10–15 minutes. until tender. Drain and rinse in cold water, then lay out to dry on a clean tea-towel.

Set the oven at 190°C / 375°F / gas 5. Place the crab meat in a bowl and shred it with two forks. If using brown meat as well as white, add it after the white has been shredded. Mix in the breadcrumbs, spring onions and ricotta, with salt and pepper.

There are two ways of filling cannelloni: either put the crab mixture into a piping bag fitted with a large plain nozzle and force the mixture into the tubes, or use a teaspoon to fill the tubes. For those who are confident about using a piping bag the former method is less messy.

Lay the filled cannelloni in the prepared baking dish or dishes. Pour the tomato sauce over. Top with the mozzarella and bake for about 40 minutes, until golden.

SERVES FOUR

PASTICCIO DI LASAGNE VERDE

fat for greasing
250 g / 9 oz green lasagne
60 ml / 4 tbsp oil
50 g / 2 oz onion, chopped
1 garlic clove, chopped
50 g / 2 oz celery, chopped
50 g / 2 oz carrot, chopped
500 g / 18 oz lean minced beef
300 ml / ½ pint beef stock
50 g / 2 oz tomato purée
salt and pepper
75 g / 3 oz walnut pieces, finely chopped
50 g / 2 oz sultanas
250 g / 9 oz tomatoes, peeled, seeded and chopped
50 g / 2 oz red pepper, seeded and chopped
150 ml / ¼ pint cold Cheese Sauce (page 230)

Grease a shallow ovenproof dish. Cook the lasagne if necessary (if using lasagne which requires no pre-cooking, follow package instructions). Leave to dry.

Heat the oil in a frying pan and cook the onion, garlic, celery and carrot for 5 minutes. Add the minced meat and brown it lightly all over. Add the stock, tomato purée and salt and pepper to taste. Bring to the boil, lower the heat and simmer for 30 minutes. Set the oven at 180°C / 350°F / gas 4.

Line the bottom of the dish with half the pasta and cover with the meat mixture, then sprinkle with the nuts, sultanas, tomatoes and red pepper. Cover with the remaining pasta. Coat with the cold sauce and bake for 20 minutes.

SERVES FOUR

MACARONI CHEESE

An old favourite, Macaroni Cheese may be served solo or
with grilled bacon or sausages. A layer of sliced tomato may
be added to the topping before being baked or grilled, if liked.

fat for greasing
150 g / 5 oz elbow macaroni
salt and pepper
600 ml / 1 pint hot White Sauce (page 230)
100 g / 4 oz Cheddar cheese, grated

Grease a 750 ml / 1¼ pint pie dish. Set the oven at 200°C / 400°F / gas 6. Cook the macaroni in a large saucepan of boiling salted water for 10–12 minutes or until tender but still firm to the bite.

Drain the macaroni thoroughly and stir it gently into the white sauce. Add three-quarters of the cheese, with salt and pepper to taste. Spoon the mixture into the prepared pie dish. Sprinkle with the remaining cheese and bake for 15–20 minutes.

Alternatively, place under a preheated grill for 2–4 minutes to melt and brown the cheese topping.

SERVES THREE TO FOUR

Dairy Foods

Dairy foods include milk, cream, cheese, yogurt, butter and eggs. They are all highly nutritious protein foods and great sources of calcium and vitamins A and D.

HOME-MADE YOGURT

Yogurt can easily be made at home. It will not always have the consistency of the commercial product, but the results will be successful if a few simple rules are followed. The yogurt will keep for 4–5 days in a refrigerator. A new carton of commercial yogurt will be needed for the next incubation.

The yogurt can be incubated in one of three ways:

- In an electric, thermostatically controlled incubator. These are very useful if the family eats a lot of yogurt.
- In a wide-necked vacuum flask (a narrow-necked flask is not suitable as the yogurt is broken up when it is removed). This is suitable for smaller quantities of yogurt.
- In a home-made incubator made from a large biscuit or cake tin with a lid. Line the base and sides with an insulating material such as woollen fabric or cotton wool and have a piece of material large enough to fit inside the top. Use 4 or 5 screw-topped glass jars that will fit inside the incubator.

METHOD

- Sterilize all the equipment by immersion in boiling water for at least 3 minutes or by using a commercial sterilizing solution.
- Heat 500 ml / 17 fl oz UHT or sterilized milk to 43°C / 108°F in a saucepan (use a cooking thermometer) and blend in 5 ml / 1 tsp fresh natural yogurt.

MICROWAVE TIP

Yogurt can be made in the microwave. Heat 600 ml / 1 pint milk in a large bowl on High for 6 minutes. Cool until tepid (about 46°C / 115°F) and stir in 15 ml / 1 tbsp plain yogurt. Add 30 ml / 2 tbsp dried full-cream powdered milk. Beat well. Cover the bowl and heat on Low for 70 minutes. Cool, then chill until required.

Alternatively, use a yogurt starter culture (obtainable with full instructions from dairy laboratories).

- Pour into pots or glasses, if using. Place in the vacuum flask or prepared incubator, seal, and leave for 6–8 hours.
- Turn the yogurt into a cold bowl and cool rapidly, standing the bowl in cold water and whisking the yogurt until creamy.
- Cover the bowl and chill for about 4 hours when the yogurt will have thickened further.
- When serving, gently stir in sugar. Flavour with stewed fruit or jam.

USING YOGURT

- Plain yogurt may be used in place of cream in savoury and sweet cooking. When heated it may curdle, so stir it into hot sauces, soups and other dishes at the end of cooking.
- Use plain yogurt in salad dressings, dips and savoury mousses.
- Yogurt combined with flour is less likely to curdle on cooking, for example in quiche fillings or as a topping for savoury bakes.
- Substitute plain yogurt for cream to give a lighter texture and sharper flavour in cold desserts.
- Spread a thick layer of plain yogurt or Greek yogurt over drained canned apricots in a shallow gratin dish. Top with a generous coating of brown sugar and flash under a hot grill to make a wonderful fruit brûlée.
- Stir clear honey into plain yogurt. Add toasted almonds just before serving.
- Make a tangy fruit jelly by dissolving a jelly tablet in a half quantity of hot water. Allow the jelly to cool before stirring it into an equal quantity of plain yogurt. Pour into a mould or individual dishes and chill until set.

SIMPLE SOFT CHEESE

Strictly speaking this is not a cheese at all – it is strained yogurt which becomes thick and similar in texture to a soft cheese. It can be used in place of soft cheese in many recipes or flavoured to serve as a spread.

1.1 litres / 2 pints yogurt or low-fat fromage frais
30 ml / 2 tbsp lemon juice

Have ready a large piece of double-thick scalded muslin. Put the yogurt or fromage frais in a bowl and stir in the lemon juice. Pour the mixture into the muslin and gather up the corners, then hang the yogurt or fromage frais overnight in a cool place.

Discard the liquid, then squeeze the muslin lightly. Use a spatula to scrape the 'cheese' into a bowl. Cover and chill.

MAKES ABOUT 225 G / 8 OZ

VARIATIONS

- Add salt and pepper to taste. Mix in chopped parsley, a little chopped fresh tarragon, some chopped fresh thyme and a little crushed garlic (if liked). Press neatly into a dish and chill until ready to serve with crackers or crusty bread.
- Mix 50 g / 2 oz finely chopped walnuts and 45 ml / 3 tbsp snipped chives into the cheese.
- Finely chop ½ seeded red pepper, then add it to the cheese with 30 ml / 2 tbsp grated onion and salt and pepper to taste.
- Make a sweet cheese by adding grated orange rind and sugar to taste.

MRS BEETON'S CHEESE PUDDINGS

75 g / 3 oz butter, melted
50 g / 2 oz fresh breadcrumbs
60 ml / 4 tbsp milk
4 eggs, separated
salt and pepper
100 g / 4 oz Cheshire cheese, finely grated
100 g / 4 oz Parmesan cheese, grated

Set the oven at 190°C / 375°F / gas 5. Grease 4 individual soufflé dishes or an ovenproof dish with some of the butter. Place the bread in a bowl and sprinkle the milk over. Leave for 5 minutes, then beat in the egg yolks, salt and pepper and both types of cheese.

Whisk the egg whites until stiff. Stir the remaining melted butter into the cheese mixture, then fold in the egg whites. Turn into the dishes and bake for about 30 minutes for individual puddings or 40–45 minutes for a large pudding. Serve at once.

SERVES FOUR

CHEESE AND POTATO PIE

fat for greasing
675 g / 1½ lb potatoes, halved
175 g / 6 oz Cheddar cheese, finely grated
salt and pepper
milk (see method)

Grease a pie dish. Cook the potatoes in a saucepan of boiling water for about 20 minutes or until tender. Drain thoroughly and mash with a potato masher, or beat with a hand-held electric whisk until smooth.

Add 150 g / 5 oz of the grated cheese, with salt and pepper to taste, then beat in milk to make a creamy mixture. Spoon into the dish, sprinkle with the remaining cheese and brown under a moderate grill for 3–5 minutes. Serve hot.

SERVES FOUR

CROQUE MONSIEUR

These classic hot ham and cheese sandwiches may be grilled or baked, in which case the outside of the sandwiches should be spread with a little butter before cooking. A little French mustard may be spread on the buttered bread when assembling the sandwiches. If a poached, baked or fried egg is served on top of the whole cooked sandwiches they become Croque Madame.

8 slices of bread, crusts removed
butter
4 thin slices of lean cooked ham
4 slices of Gruyère cheese

Spread the bread with butter and make 4 ham and cheese sandwiches, pressing them together firmly.

Heat a knob of butter in a large frying pan and fry the sandwiches for about 2 minutes on each side, until crisp and golden. Transfer to a platter and cut diagonally in half or into quarters.

SERVES FOUR

MRS BEETON'S BAKED CHEESE SANDWICHES

8 slices of bread
butter
4 large thick slices of Cheshire or Cheddar cheese

Set the oven at 200°C / 400°F / gas 6 and heat a baking sheet. Spread the bread with the butter and make 4 cheese sandwiches.

Spread the top of each sandwich very lightly with butter, then invert them on the hot baking sheet. Spread the top of each sandwich very lightly with butter. Bake for 5 minutes, turn the sandwiches and bake for a further 5 minutes, until golden. Serve at once.

SERVES FOUR

TOASTED CHEESE

A traditional savoury to serve at the end of the meal, this would have been kept hot at the table in a hot-water cheese dish, which consisted of a metal container (for the cheese) set over a reservoir of hot water.

175 g / 6 oz mature Cheddar cheese, grated
5–10 ml / 1–2 tsp prepared English mustard
freshly-ground black pepper
15–30 ml / 1–2 tbsp port
hot toast to serve

Heat the grill. Place the cheese in a bowl over a saucepan of simmering water. Stir occasionally until melted, then add the mustard, pepper and port to taste. Pour into a flameproof dish and brown the top under the grill. Serve at once with hot toast.

SERVES FOUR

EGGY BREAD AND CHEESE

8 thin slices of white bread, crusts removed
butter
175 g / 6 oz Cheshire or Cheddar cheese, thinly sliced
3 eggs, beaten
salt
oil for shallow frying

Spread the bread thinly with butter. Top four of the slices with cheese, leaving a narrow border all around. Add the remaining slices of bread to make four sandwiches, then press the edges of each sandwich lightly with a rolling pin to seal in the filling.

Put the eggs with a little salt in a shallow dish large enough to hold all the sandwiches in a single layer. Add the sandwiches and soak for 20 minutes, turning them over carefully halfway through.

Heat the oil in a large frying pan, add the sandwiches and fry for 2–3 minutes on each side until crisp and golden. Drain on absorbent kitchen paper before serving.

SERVES FOUR

YORKSHIRE PUDDING BATTER

*Yorkshire pudding can be made in a large baking tin
or in individual tins. For more information see Roast Ribs
of Beef with Yorkshire Pudding on pages 80–1.*

**100 g / 4 oz plain flour
pinch of salt
1 egg, beaten
150 ml / ¼ pint milk**

Sift the flour into a bowl and add a pinch of salt. Make a well in the centre and add the beaten egg. Stir in the milk, gradually working in the flour. Beat vigorously until the mixture is smooth and bubbly, then stir in 150 ml / ¼ pint water. Pour into a jug. The mixture may be left to stand at this stage, in which case it should be covered and stored in the refrigerator.

MAKES ABOUT 300 ML / ½ PINT

COATING BATTER

This is a stiff batter, suitable for cod fillets, meat, poultry or other firm foods.

**100 g / 4 oz plain flour
pinch of salt
1 egg
125 ml / 4 fl oz milk**

Sift the flour and salt into a bowl and make a well in the centre.

Add the egg and a little milk, then beat well, gradually incorporating the flour and the remaining milk to make a smooth batter.

MAKES ABOUT 150 ML / ¼ PINT

LIGHT BATTER

This light, thin batter is ideal for delicate or sweet foods.

100 g / 4 oz plain flour
pinch of salt
15 ml / 1 tbsp oil
2 egg whites

Sift the flour and salt into a bowl and make a well in the centre.

Pour 125 ml / 4 fl oz cold water into the well in the flour and add the oil. Gradually beat the liquid into the flour to make a smooth, thick batter. Beat really well so that the batter is light.

Just before the batter is to be used, whisk the egg whites until stiff in a clean dry bowl. Fold the egg whites into the batter and use at once.

MAKES ABOUT 175 ML / 6 FL OZ

EVERYDAY PANCAKES

*Pancakes are much too good to be reserved exclusively
for Shrove Tuesday. Simple, versatile, and always popular,
they lend themselves to a wide range of savoury and sweet fillings.*

**100 g / 4 oz plain flour
1.25 ml / ¼ tsp salt
1 egg, beaten
250 ml / 8 fl oz milk, or half milk and half water
oil for frying**

Make the batter. Sift the flour and salt into a bowl, make a well in the centre
and add the beaten egg. Stir in half the milk (or all the milk, if using a mixture
of milk and water), gradually working the flour down from the sides.

Beat vigorously until the mixture is smooth and bubbly, then stir in the rest of
the milk (or the water). Pour into a jug. The mixture may be left to stand at this
stage, in which case it should be covered and stored in the refrigerator.

Heat a little oil in a clean 18 cm / 7 inch pancake pan. Pour off any excess oil,
leaving the pan covered with a thin film of grease. Stir the batter and pour about
30–45 ml / 2–3 tbsp into the pan. There should be just enough to thinly cover
the base. Tilt and rotate the pan so that the batter runs over the surface evenly.

Cook over a moderate heat for about 1 minute until the pancake is set and
golden brown underneath. Make sure the pancake is loose by shaking the pan,
then either toss it or turn it quickly with a palette knife or fish slice. Cook the
second side for about 30 seconds or until golden.

Slide the pancake out on to a warmed plate. Serve at once, with a suitable filling or sauce, or keep warm over simmering water while making 7 more
pancakes in the same way. Add more oil to the pan when necessary.

MAKES EIGHT

VARIATIONS

- **Rich Pancakes** Add 15 g / ½ oz cooled melted butter or 15 ml / 1 tbsp oil to the batter with 1 egg yolk. Alternatively, enrich the batter by adding 1 whole egg.
- **Cream Pancakes** Use 150 ml / ¼ pint milk and 50 ml / 2 fl oz single cream instead of 250 ml / 8 fl oz milk. Add 2 eggs and 25 g / 1 oz cooled melted butter, then stir in 15 ml / 1 tbsp brandy with caster sugar to taste. The mixture should only just coat the back of a spoon as the pancakes should be very thin.

SAVOURY PANCAKE FILLINGS

Reheat savoury pancakes in a 180°C / 350°F / gas 4 oven for 30 minutes if they have a cold filling; 20 minutes if the filling is hot. Pancakes topped with grated cheese may be browned under the grill.

- **Asparagus** Add 30 ml / 2 tbsp thawed frozen chopped spinach to the pancake batter, if liked. Place a trimmed slice of ham on each pancake, top with a large asparagus spear and roll up. Cover the rolled pancakes with 600 ml / 1 pint Béchamel sauce (page 232), reheat, then sprinkle with grated Gruyère cheese and grill to brown.
- **Chicken and Mushroom** Sauté 175 g / 6 oz sliced mushrooms in 45 ml / 3 tbsp butter for 2–3 minutes. Stir in 15 ml / 1 tbsp plain flour and cook for 1 minute, then gradually add 150 ml / ¼ pint chicken stock. Bring to the boil, stirring. Add 5 ml / 1 tsp mushroom ketchup, if liked. Stir in 75 g / 3 oz chopped cooked chicken. Fill the pancakes and reheat.
- **Poached Haddock** Poach 300 g / 11 oz smoked haddock fillets in a little water for 10–15 minutes. Drain and flake the fish. Make 250 ml / 8 fl oz Béchamel sauce (page 232). Add the fish and 2 chopped hard-boiled eggs, 5 ml / 1 tsp chopped capers, 5 ml / 1 tbsp chopped parsley, 15 ml / 1 tbsp lemon juice and salt and pepper. Fill the pancakes, sprinkle with 25 g / 1 oz grated cheese and reheat.
- **Spinach Pancakes** Cook 300 g / 11 oz frozen spinach; drain well. Add 200 g / 7 oz cottage cheese, 50 g / 2 oz grated mature Cheddar cheese; 100 ml / 3½ fl oz double cream, a pinch of nutmeg and seasoning. Fill the pancakes, sprinkle with 25 g / 1 oz grated cheese and reheat.

SWEET PANCAKE FILLINGS

Lemon juice and caster sugar share the honours with warmed jam as the most common fillings for pancakes. Here are a few more ideas: Spoon the chosen filling on to the pancakes and roll up. If liked, sprinkle the rolled pancakes with caster sugar, and glaze in a very hot oven or under a hot grill.

- **Apple** In a bowl, mix together 250 ml / 8 fl oz sweetened thick apple purée, 50 g / 2 oz sultanas and a pinch of cinnamon.
- **Apricot** Add 15 ml / 1 tbsp cinnamon to the batter when making the pancakes. Soak 50 g / 2 oz dried apricots in 60 ml / 4 tbsp water in a saucepan, then simmer with 50 g / 2 oz sugar and a generous squeeze of lemon juice until soft and pulpy. Add 25 g / 1 oz chopped toasted almonds.
- **Banana** In a bowl, mash 4 bananas with 50 g / 2 oz softened butter, 30 ml / 2 tbsp sugar and the grated rind and juice of 1 lemon.
- **Chocolate and Whipped Cream** Whip 150 ml / ¼ pint double cream with 15–30 ml / 1–2 tbsp icing sugar until it stands in soft peaks. Gently fold in 100 g / 4 oz grated chocolate and 30 ml / 2 tbsp finely chopped toasted hazelnuts. Swirl this on the pancakes, fold into quarters and serve at once.
- **Curd Cheese** In a bowl, beat 100 g / 4 oz curd cheese with 45 ml / 3 tbsp double cream, 30 ml / 2 tbsp caster sugar and the grated rind of ½ lemon. Add 40 g / 1½ oz sultanas.
- **Dried Fruit** Put 100 g / 4 oz chopped raisins, dates and cut mixed peel into a small saucepan with 100 ml / 3 ½ fl oz apple juice. Simmer until syrupy.
- **Ginger and Banana** Add 15 ml / 1 tbsp ground ginger to the batter when making the pancakes, if liked. For the filling, mash 4 bananas in a bowl with 30 ml / 2 tbsp double cream. Add a few pieces of chopped preserved ginger.
- **Maple Syrup and Ice Cream** Trickle about 10 ml / 2 tsp maple syrup over each pancake and roll up. Arrange on serving plates and top with good-quality Cornish ice cream. Sprinkle with chopped walnuts.
- **Pineapple** Drain 1 (227 g / 8 oz) can crushed pineapple. Combine the fruit with 250 ml / 8 fl oz soured cream in a bowl. Fill the pancakes with this mixture and serve with a sauce made by heating the fruit syrup with a few drops of lemon juice.
- **Rum Warmers** Place 45 ml / 3 tbsp brown sugar in a saucepan with 5 ml / 1 tsp ground cinnamon and 90 ml / 6 tbsp orange juice. Heat until the sugar melts, then bring to the boil and boil for 1 minute. Remove from the heat and stir in 60 ml / 4 tbsp rum. Moisten the pancakes with a little rum syrup before rolling them up, then trickle the remainder over the top. Serve with whipped cream.
- **Surprise** Spoon ice cream into the centre of each pancake and fold in half like an omelette. Serve at once with a jam sauce.

EGGS IN COCOTTES

25 g / 1 oz butter
4 eggs
salt and pepper
60 ml / 4 tbsp milk or cream

Butter 4 ramekins or cocottes at least 3.5 cm / 1¼ inches deep, and stand them in a baking tin containing enough warm water to come halfway up their sides. Set the oven at 180°C / 350°F / gas 4.

Break an egg into each warm dish and add salt and pepper to taste. Top with any remaining butter, cut into flakes. Spoon 15 ml / 1 tbsp milk or cream over each egg.

Bake for 6–10 minutes, depending on the thickness of the dishes. The whites of the eggs should be just set. Wipe the outsides of the dishes and serve at once.

SERVES FOUR

VARIATIONS

- Shake ground nutmeg or cayenne pepper over the eggs before cooking.
- Sprinkle the eggs with very finely grated cheese before cooking.
- Put sliced, fried mushrooms, chopped ham, cooked diced chicken or lightly sautéed, diced Italian sausage in the bottom of each dish before adding the eggs.
- Put 15–30 ml / 1–2 tbsp spinach purée in the dishes before adding the eggs.

APPLE FRITTERS

450 g / 1 lb apples
5 ml / 1 tsp lemon juice
oil for deep frying
caster sugar for sprinkling
single cream to serve

BATTER
100 g / 4 oz plain flour
1.25 ml / ¼ tsp salt
15 ml / 1 tbsp vegetable oil
60 ml / 4 tbsp milk
2 egg whites

Make the batter. Sift the flour and salt into a bowl. Make a well in the centre of the flour and add the oil and milk. Gradually work in the flour from the sides, then beat well until smooth. Stir in 75 ml / 5 tbsp cold water. The mixture may be left to stand at this stage, in which case it should be covered and stored in the refrigerator.

Peel and core the apples. Cut them into 5 mm / ¼ inch slices and place in a bowl of cold water with the lemon juice added.

Whisk the egg whites in a clean, grease-free bowl until stiff. Give the batter a final beat, then lightly fold in the egg whites.

Set the oven at 150°C / 300°F / gas 2. Put the oil for frying in a deep wide saucepan. Heat the oil to 185°C / 360°F or until a bread cube immersed in the oil turns pale brown in 45 seconds. If using a deep-fat fryer, follow the manufacturer's instructions.

Drain the apples thoroughly and dry with soft absorbent kitchen paper. Coat the apple slices in batter and fry 5 or 6 pieces at a time for 2–3 minutes until golden. Lift out the fritters with a slotted spoon and dry on absorbent kitchen paper. Keep hot on a baking sheet in the oven while cooking the next batch.

When all the fritters have been cooked, sprinkle them with caster sugar and serve with cream.

SERVES FOUR

VARIATIONS

- **Apricot Fritters** Prepare batter as above. Sprinkle drained canned apricot halves with rum and leave for 15 minutes. Coat in batter, then fry. Dredge with caster sugar and serve with custard or cream.

- **Banana Fritters** Prepare batter as above. Peel 4 small bananas, cut in half lengthways, then in half across. Coat in batter, then fry. Serve with custard or liqueur-flavoured cream.

- **Orange Fritters** Prepare batter as above. Remove the peel and pith from 4 oranges. Divide them into pieces of about 2 or 3 segments each. Carefully cut into the centre to remove any pips. Coat in batter, then fry. Serve with custard or cream.

- **Pear Fritters** Prepare batter as above. Peel and core 4 pears. Cut into quarters, sprinkle with sugar and kirsch and leave to stand for 15 minutes. Finely crush 4 almond macaroons and toss the pear pieces in the crumbs. Coat in batter, then fry. Serve with a lemon sauce.

- **Pineapple Fritters** Prepare batter as above. Drain 1 (556 g / 19 oz) can pineapple rings, pat dry on absorbent kitchen paper, and sprinkle with 20 ml / 4 tsp kirsch. Leave to stand for 15 minutes. Coat in batter, then fry. Serve with the pineapple juice, thickened with arrowroot.

EGGS A LA MAITRE D'HOTEL

100 g / 4 oz butter
30 ml / 2 tbsp plain flour
300 ml / ½ pint milk
salt and pepper
30 ml / 2 tbsp chopped parsley
6 eggs, hard boiled and quartered
juice of ½ lemon

Melt half the butter in a small saucepan. Stir in the flour and cook for a few seconds, then gradually pour in the milk, stirring all the time. Bring to the boil, stirring, reduce the heat and leave the sauce to simmer gently for 5 minutes. Gradually beat in the remaining butter, add the parsley and remove from the heat.

Arrange the eggs in a dish or in four individual dishes. Stir the lemon juice into the sauce, pour it over the eggs and serve.

SERVES FOUR

OEUFS AU PLAT

50 g / 2 oz butter
4 eggs
salt and white pepper

Set the oven at 180°C / 350°F / gas 4 or heat the grill. Butter a shallow oven-proof or flameproof dish (for grilling) quite generously. The lid of an ovenproof glass casserole or a medium quiche dish will do instead of a gratin dish.

Break the eggs into the dish and sprinkle with salt and white pepper. Dot with the remaining butter. Bake for about 12 minutes, or until the eggs are cooked to taste. Alternatively, place them under the grill on a low rack. Cook for about 5 minutes, or until the eggs are set.

SERVES FOUR

PEASANTS' EGGS

salt and pepper
575 g / 1¼ lb potatoes, cubed
60 ml / 4 tbsp oil
8 rindless back bacon rashers, cut into strips
1 onion, chopped
30 ml / 2 tbsp chopped parsley
30 ml / 2 tbsp butter
4 eggs

Bring a large saucepan of salted water to the boil, add the potatoes and bring back to the boil. Cook for 1 minute, then drain thoroughly.

Heat the oil in a large deep frying pan. Add the bacon and fry for 2–3 minutes until crisp. Using a slotted spoon, remove and drain on absorbent kitchen paper. Add the onion to the oil remaining in the pan and fry for 3–4 minutes until golden; remove with the slotted spoon and put in the baking dish with the bacon. Keep hot.

Add the potatoes to the frying pan and fry gently for 5–6 minutes, turning occasionally, until cooked and brown. Drain and add to the bacon and onion mixture with plenty of salt, pepper and parsley. Mix lightly and keep hot.

Melt the butter in the remaining oil. Fry the eggs. Arrange on the potato mixture and serve at once.

SERVES FOUR

EGGS FLORENTINE

butter for greasing
1 kg / 2¼ lb fresh spinach or 2 (225 g / 8 oz) packets frozen leaf spinach
15 ml / 1 tbsp butter
salt and pepper
4 eggs
100 g / 4 oz Fontina or Cheddar cheese, finely grated

Set the oven at 190°C / 375°F / gas 5. Wash the fresh spinach several times and remove any coarse stalks. Put into a saucepan with just the water that clings to the leaves, then cover the pan with a tight-fitting lid. Place over moderate heat for about 3 minutes, shaking the pan often until the spinach has wilted. Lower the heat slightly and cook for 3–5 minutes more. (Cook frozen spinach according to the directions on the packet.)

When the spinach is tender, drain it thoroughly in a colander. Cut through the leaves several times with a knife to chop them roughly. Melt the butter in the clean pan, add the spinach with salt and pepper to taste, and heat through gently.

Spoon into a greased ovenproof dish and, using the back of a spoon, make 4 small hollows in the surface. Break an egg into each hollow, add salt and pepper to taste, then sprinkle the grated cheese over the eggs. Bake for 12–15 minutes until the eggs are lightly set. Serve at once.

SERVES FOUR

CURRIED EGGS

60 ml / 4 tbsp oil
2 onions, finely chopped
1 cooking apple
15–30 ml / 1–2 tbsp mild curry powder
30 ml / 2 tbsp plain flour
10 ml / 2 tsp tomato purée
500 ml / 17 fl oz vegetable stock
30 ml / 2 tbsp mango chutney
15 ml / 1 tbsp soft light brown sugar
30 ml / 2 tbsp lemon juice
salt
6 eggs, hard boiled, shelled and cut into quarters
30 ml / 2 tbsp plain yogurt

Heat the oil in a saucepan, add the onions and sautée for 4–6 minutes until soft but not coloured. Peel, core and chop the apple. Add it to the onions, and continue cooking for 5 minutes.

Stir in the curry powder and flour and fry for 2–3 minutes, then add the tomato purée, vegetable stock, chutney, sugar, lemon juice and a pinch of salt. Bring to the boil, stirring constantly, then lower the heat, cover and simmer for 30 minutes, stirring occasionally.

Add the hard-boiled eggs and warm through over gentle heat. To serve, remove from the heat and gently stir in the yogurt, taking care not to break up the curried eggs.

SERVES FOUR

MRS BEETON'S TIP

Cook some Basmati rice according to the instructions on page 168, adding a few frozen peas halfway through cooking. Serve the rice and peas with the eggs.

EGGS BENEDICT

2 muffins, split, or 4 slices of white bread
30 ml / 2 tbsp butter
4 slices of ham
4 eggs

HOLLANDAISE SAUCE
45 ml / 3 tbsp white wine vinegar
6 peppercorns
½ bay leaf
1 blade of mace
3 egg yolks
100 g / 4 oz butter, softened
salt and pepper

Make the Hollandaise sauce. Combine the vinegar, peppercorns, bay leaf and mace in a small saucepan. Boil rapidly until the liquid is reduced to 15 ml / 1 tbsp. Strain into a heatproof bowl and leave to cool. Add the egg yolks and a nut of butter to the vinegar and place over a saucepan of gently simmering water. Heat the mixture gently, beating constantly until thick. Do not allow it to approach boiling point. Add the remaining butter, a little at a time, beating well after each addition. When all the butter has been added the sauce should be thick and glossy. Season lightly.

Toast the muffins or bread slices, then butter them. Trim the ham slices to fit the bread. Put the trimmings on the hot muffins or toast and cover with the ham slices. Put on a large heated platter or individual plates and keep hot.

Poach the eggs and drain well. Put an egg on each piece of ham, cover with about 15 ml / 1 tbsp of the Hollandaise sauce and serve the remaining sauce separately.

SERVES FOUR

OMELETTE

*The secret of a light omelette is to add water, not milk, to the mixture,
beating it only sufficiently to mix the yolks and whites. The mixture must
be cooked quickly until evenly and lightly set, then served when still moist.
Have everything ready before you start to cook, including the diner so
that the omelette can be taken to the table as soon as it is ready.*

**2 eggs
salt and pepper
15 ml / 1 tbsp unsalted butter or margarine**

Break the eggs into a bowl, add 15 ml / 1 tbsp cold water, salt and pepper. Beat lightly with a fork. Thoroughly heat a frying pan or omelette pan. When it is hot, add the butter or margarine, tilting the pan so that the whole surface is lightly greased. Without drawing the pan off the heat, add the egg mixture. Leave to stand for 10 seconds.

Using a spatula, gently draw the egg mixture from the sides to the centre as it sets, allowing the uncooked egg mixture to run in to fill the gap. Do not stir or the mixture will scramble.

When the omelette is golden and set underneath, but still slightly moist on top, remove it from the heat. Loosen the edges by shaking the pan, using a round-bladed knife or the edge of a spatula, then flip one-third of the omelette towards the centre. Flip the opposite third over towards the centre. Tip the omelette on to a hot plate, folded sides underneath. Alternatively, the cooked omelette may be rolled out of the pan after the first folding, so that it is served folded in three. A simpler method is to fold the omelette in half in the pan, then slide it out on to the plate.

SERVES ONE

FILLINGS

- **Cheese** Add 40 g / 1½ oz grated cheese to the beaten eggs. Sprinkle a further 15 g / ½ oz over the omelette.

continues overleaf ...

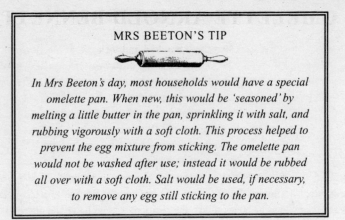

MRS BEETON'S TIP

In Mrs Beeton's day, most households would have a special omelette pan. When new, this would be 'seasoned' by melting a little butter in the pan, sprinkling it with salt, and rubbing vigorously with a soft cloth. This process helped to prevent the egg mixture from sticking. The omelette pan would not be washed after use; instead it would be rubbed all over with a soft cloth. Salt would be used, if necessary, to remove any egg still sticking to the pan.

- **Fines Herbes** Add 2.5 ml / ½ tsp chopped fresh tarragon, 2.5 ml / ½ tsp chopped fresh chervil, 5 ml / 1 tsp chopped parsley and a few snipped chives to the beaten eggs.
- **Ham** Add 50 g / 2 oz chopped ham to the egg mixture.
- **Fish** Add 50 g / 2 oz flaked cooked fish to the omelette just before folding.
- **Bacon** Grill 2 rindless bacon rashers until crisp; crumble into the centre of the omelette just before folding.
- **Mushroom** Fry 50 g / 2 oz sliced mushrooms in butter. Spoon into the centre of the omelette just before folding.
- **Shrimp or Prawn Sautée** 50 g / 2 oz shrimps or prawns in a little butter in a saucepan. Add a squeeze of lemon juice and spoon into the omelette before folding.
- **Chicken** Chop 25 g / 1 oz cooked chicken. Mix with 60 ml / 4 tbsp white sauce. Heat gently in a small saucepan. Spoon into the centre of the omelette before folding.

OMELETTE ARNOLD BENNETT

150 g / 5 oz smoked haddock
25 g / 1 oz unsalted butter
60 ml / 4 tbsp single cream
2 eggs, separated
salt and pepper
30 ml / 2 tbsp grated Parmesan cheese
parsley sprigs to garnish

Bring a saucepan of water to simmering point, add the haddock and poach gently for 10 minutes. Using a slotted spoon transfer the fish to a large plate. Remove any skin or bones. Flake the fish into a large bowl and add half the butter and 15 ml / 1 tbsp of the cream. Mix well.

In a separate bowl mix the egg yolks with 15 ml / 1 tbsp of the remaining cream. Add salt and pepper to taste. Add to the fish mixture and stir in half the cheese.

In a clean dry bowl, whisk the egg whites until stiff. Fold them into the fish mixture.

Heat half the remaining butter in an omelette pan. Pour in half the fish mixture and cook quickly until golden brown underneath (see Mrs Beeton's Tip). Sprinkle over half the remaining cheese, spoon over 15 ml / 1 tbsp of the remaining cream and brown quickly under a hot grill. Do not fold. Very quickly make a second omelette in the same way. Garnish and serve at once.

SERVES TWO

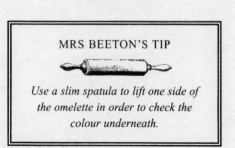

MRS BEETON'S TIP

Use a slim spatula to lift one side of
the omelette in order to check the
colour underneath.

SPANISH OMELETTE

*Known as tortilla, a Spanish omelette is quite different from filled
and folded omelettes or featherlight soufflé omelettes. It is a thick cake
of potato and onion set in eggs, cut into wedges and served hot or cold.
This classic potato omelette is quite delicious without any additional
ingredients; however, the recipe is often varied to include red and green
peppers or a mixture of vegetables, such as peas and green beans.*

675 g / 1½ lb potatoes
225 g / 8 oz onions, thinly sliced
salt and pepper
45 ml / 3 tbsp olive oil
6 eggs, beaten

Cut the potatoes into 1 cm / ½ inch cubes and mix them with the onions in a
basin. Add plenty of seasoning and mix well.

Heat the oil in a heavy-bottomed frying pan which has fairly deep sides. Add
the potatoes and onions, then cook, stirring and turning the vegetables often,
until both potatoes and onions are tender. This takes about 25 minutes.

Pour the eggs over the potatoes and cook over medium heat, stirring, until the
eggs begin to set. Press the vegetables down evenly and leave to set. Lower the
heat to prevent the base of the omelette overbrowning before the eggs have set
sufficiently.

Lay a large plate over the omelette and invert the pan to turn the omelette out
on the plate. The base of the pan should be well greased but if it looks a little
dry, then add a little extra olive oil and heat it. Slide the omelette back into the
pan and cook over medium to high heat for 3–5 minutes, until crisp and
browned. Serve the omelette hot, warm or cold.

SERVES FOUR TO SIX

Pizza and Dough Bakes

ITALIAN-STYLE PIZZA

*This should be thin and crisp with a
slightly bubbly dough base and a moist topping.*

**fat for greasing
25 g / 1 oz fresh yeast or 15 ml / 1 tbsp dried yeast
5 ml / 1 tsp sugar
450 g / 1 lb strong white flour
5 ml / 1 tsp salt
30 ml / 2 tbsp olive oil
flour for rolling out**

TOPPING
**60 ml / 4 tbsp olive oil
2 garlic cloves, crushed
1 large onion, chopped
15 ml / 1 tbsp dried oregano or marjoram
1 (397 g / 14 oz) can chopped tomatoes
30 ml / 2 tbsp tomato purée
salt and pepper
375 g / 12 oz mozzarella cheese, sliced**

Grease four large baking sheets. Measure 300 ml / ½ pint lukewarm water. Blend the fresh yeast with the sugar and a little lukewarm water. Set aside until frothy. For dried yeast, sprinkle the yeast over all the water, then leave until frothy.

Sift the flour and salt into a bowl, make a well in the middle and add the yeast liquid, any remaining water and oil. Mix the flour into the liquid to make a firm dough.

Turn out the dough on to a lightly floured surface and knead thoroughly until smooth and elastic – about 10 minutes. Place the dough in a clean, lightly floured bowl. Cover with cling film and leave in a warm place until doubled in bulk. This will take about 2 hours.

To make the topping, heat the oil in a saucepan and cook the garlic and onion until soft but not browned – about 15 minutes. Stir in the oregano, tomatoes and tomato purée. Bring to the boil, reduce the heat and simmer for 15 minutes. Remove the pan from the heat and add salt and pepper to taste.

Set the oven at 240ºC / 475ºF / gas 9. Knead the dough again, then divide it into four. Roll out each portion into a 25–30 cm / 10–12 inch circle. Place a piece of dough on each prepared baking sheet. Top with the tomato mixture and mozzarella, then leave in a warm place for about 5 minutes, or until the dough bases begin to rise slightly.

Bake for about 15 minutes, or until the topping is well browned and the dough is crisp and bubbly. Serve freshly baked.

MAKES FOUR

CALZONE

*A type of pizza pasty, calzone is a pizza which is folded in half
to enclose its filling. Often filled with a meat sauce (bolognese)
and mozzarella, the filling may be varied according to taste.*

fat for greasing
25 g / 1 oz fresh yeast or 15 ml / 1 tbsp dried yeast
5 ml / 1 tsp sugar
450 g / 1 lb strong white flour
5 ml / 1 tsp salt
30 ml / 2 tbsp olive oil
flour for rolling out

FILLING
225 g / 8 oz minced beef
salt and pepper
2.5 ml / ½ tsp chilli powder
1 quantity tomato pizza topping (see pages 218–9)
50 g / 2 oz mushrooms, sliced
225 g / 8 oz mozzarella cheese, sliced

Grease two baking sheets. Using the yeast, sugar, flour, salt and olive oil, with
water as required, make the dough following the recipe for Italian-style Pizza
(pages 218–9) and leave it to rise.

Meanwhile make the filling. Dry-fry the mince in a heavy-bottomed saucepan
over medium heat until well browned. If the meat is very lean you may have to
add a little olive oil. Add salt, pepper and the chilli powder. Stir in the tomato
topping and bring to the boil. Cover, lower the heat and simmer the mixture
very gently for about 30 minutes. Set aside to cool. Stir in the mushrooms when
the meat has cooled, just before the filling is to be used.

Set the oven at 220°C / 425°F / gas 7. Knead the dough again, then divide it into
quarters. Roll out one portion into a 23 cm / 9 inch circle. Place it on a prepared
baking sheet. Top one side with about a quarter of the meat mixture and a quarter of the mozzarella. Fold over the other half of the dough and pinch the edges
together firmly to seal in the filling.

Repeat with the remaining portions of dough and filling. Use the second baking sheet to fill the second calzone, then slide it on to the first sheet next to the first calzone. To shape the last calzone, sprinkle a little flour over the calzone on the baking sheet, then lift the final portion of dough on to the sheet, allowing one half to drape over the filled calzone while filling the opposite side. Otherwise the large calzone can be difficult to lift once filled.

Leave the filled dough to rise in a warm place for about 5 minutes. Bake for 30–40 minutes, or until the dough is golden, risen and cooked. Leave to stand on the baking sheets for a few minutes, then transfer to individual plates.

MAKES FOUR

FILLING IDEAS

- Courgette and Two Cheeses Make the tomato pizza topping (pages 218–9). Top the calzone first with the tomato mixture, then add courgette slices (allow 1 small courgette for each calzone) and mozzarella cheese. Sprinkle with grated Parmesan cheese and finish as in the main recipe.
- **Ham and Olive Calzone** Spread half the prepared dough with ricotta cheese, then top with a slice of ham. Add a couple of onion slices and 4 halved, pitted black olives.
- Salami Calzone Make the tomato pizza topping (pages 218–9). Top the calzone first with the tomato mixture, then add 4 slices of salami, overlapping them to fit half the dough, and mozzarella cheese. Finish as in the main recipe.

SCONE PIZZA

fat for greasing
225 g / 8 oz self-raising flour
10 ml / 2 tsp baking powder
salt and pepper
50 g / 2 oz margarine
5 ml / 1 tsp dried marjoram
2.5 ml / ½ tsp dried thyme
150 ml / ¼ pint milk

TOPPING
1 (200 g / 7 oz) can tuna in oil
1 onion, chopped
1 garlic clove (optional)
15 ml / 1 tbsp roughly chopped capers
30 ml / 2 tbsp chopped parsley
4 large tomatoes, peeled and sliced
100 g / 4 oz Cheddar cheese, grated

Grease a large baking sheet. Set the oven at 220°C / 425°F / gas 7. Sift the flour, baking powder and salt into a bowl, then rub in the margarine. Stir in the herbs and milk to make a soft dough. Knead the dough lightly.

Roll out the dough on a lightly floured surface into a 30 cm / 12 inch circle. Lift the dough on to the prepared baking sheet and turn the edges over slightly.

Drain the oil from the tuna into a small saucepan and heat it gently. Add the onion and garlic (if used) and cook for about 10 minutes, until the onion is just beginning to soften. Off the heat, add the capers, parsley and flaked tuna. Spread this topping over the scone base, cover with tomato slices, then sprinkle with the cheese.

Bake for 20–25 minutes, until the topping is bubbling and the base is risen, browned around the edges and cooked through. Serve cut into wedges.

SERVES FOUR TO SIX

EMPANADAS

fat for greasing
15 g / ½ oz fresh yeast or 10 ml / 2 tsp dried yeast
5 ml / 1 tsp sugar
225 g / 8 oz strong white flour
2.5 ml / ½ tsp salt
15 ml / 1 tbsp olive oil
flour for rolling out

FILLING
30 ml / 2 tbsp oil
1 small onion, chopped
1 green chilli, seeded and chopped
1 garlic clove, crushed
225 g / 8 oz minced beef
15 ml / 1 tbsp ground cumin
25 g / 1 oz raisins
2 tomatoes, peeled and chopped
salt and pepper

Grease a baking sheet. Make the dough following the recipe for Italian-style Pizza (pages 218–9) and leave it to rise.

To make the filling, heat the oil in a frying pan and gently cook the onion, chilli and garlic for about 15 minutes, until the onion has softened. Remove the pan from the heat, then add the mince, cumin, raisins and tomatoes. Add salt and pepper to taste and stir well.

Set the oven at 200°C / 400°F / gas 6. Knead the dough again and divide it into quarters. On a lightly floured surface, roll out one portion into a 15–18 cm / 6–7 inch round. Mound a quarter of the meat mixture on one half, leaving a space around the edge of the dough. Dampen the dough edge, then fold the dough to make a semi-circular pasty. Pinch the edges of the dough to seal in the filling, then place on the baking sheet. Make three more empanadas. Cover with cling film and leave for 5 minutes, so that the dough begins to rise. Bake for 30–40 minutes, until golden brown.

MAKES FOUR

ONION TRAY BAKE

This German-style bake is delicious hot or cold.

fat for greasing
25 g / 1 oz fresh yeast or 15 ml / 1 tbsp dried yeast
5 ml / 1 tsp sugar
450 g / 1 lb strong white flour
5 ml / 1 tsp salt
30 ml / 2 tbsp olive oil
flour for rolling out

TOPPING
25 g / 1 oz butter
450 g / 1 lb onions, thinly sliced
15 ml / 1 tbsp caraway seeds
salt and pepper
225 g / 8 oz quark or curd cheese

Grease a 33 x 23 cm / 13 x 9 inch oblong baking tin. Make the dough following the recipe for Italian-style Pizza (pages 218–9) and leave it to rise.

To make the topping, melt the butter in a large frying pan and cook the onions and caraway seeds, stirring often, for about 10 minutes, until the onions have softened slightly. Add salt and pepper to taste, then set aside.

Set the oven at 220°C / 425°F / gas 7. On a lightly floured surface, knead the dough again, then roll out to fit the tin. Press the dough into the tin, then spread the quark or curd cheese over it. Top with the onions, spreading them in an even layer and pressing down lightly. Leave the dough in a warm place for about 15 minutes, until beginning to rise.

Bake for about 30 minutes, until golden brown. Allow the bake to stand for 5–10 minutes before serving, cut into oblong portions. Alternatively, the tray bake may be left until just warm or served cold.

SERVES EIGHT

Salad
Dressings,
Marinades,
Stuffings &
Savoury
Sauces

FRENCH DRESSING

salt and pepper
pinch of mustard powder
pinch of caster sugar
30 ml / 2 tbsp wine vinegar
90 ml / 6 tbsp olive oil or a mixture of olive and sunflower oil

Mix the salt and pepper, mustard and sugar in a small bowl. Add the vinegar and whisk until the sugar has dissolved. Whisk in the oil and check the dressing for salt and pepper before using.

MAKES ABOUT 125 ML / 4 FL OZ

VARIATIONS

- Almost every cook has his or her favourite way of preparing French dressing. Garlic, whole or crushed, is a favourite addition, while others swear that a few drops of soy sauce sharpen the flavour. Lemon juice frequently replaces all or part of the vinegar. The recipe above may be doubled or trebled, if liked, but the proportions should always remain the same.

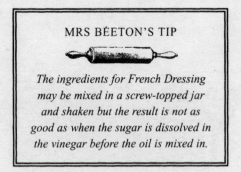

MRS BEETON'S TIP

The ingredients for French Dressing may be mixed in a screw-topped jar and shaken but the result is not as good as when the sugar is dissolved in the vinegar before the oil is mixed in.

RED WINE MARINADE

1 onion, chopped
1 carrot, chopped
1 celery stick, chopped
6–10 parsley sprigs, chopped
1 garlic clove, crushed
5 ml / 1 tsp dried thyme
1 bay leaf
6–8 peppercorns
1–2 cloves
5 ml / 1 tsp ground coriander
2.5 ml / 1 tsp juniper berries, lightly crushed
salt and pepper
250 ml / 8 fl oz rich beef stock
150 ml / ¼ pint red wine
150 ml / ¼ pint oil

Mix all the ingredients in a large bowl. Stir in 150 ml / ¼ pint water. Use as required.

MAKES ABOUT 600 ML / 1 PINT

MAITRE D'HOTEL BUTTER

100 g / 4 oz butter
4–5 large parsley sprigs, finely chopped
salt and pepper
2.5 ml / ½ tsp lemon juice

Beat the butter until creamy in a small bowl. Add the parsley, a little at a time, beating until well combined. Add salt to taste and a small pinch of pepper. Add a few drops of lemon juice to intensify the flavour. Use at once or press into small pots, tapping the pots while filling to knock out all the air. Cover with foil and refrigerate until required. Use within 2 days.

MAKES 100 G / 4 OZ

DEVILLED BUTTER

A pat of this butter, placed on fish steaks while grilling,
imparts a delicious flavour.

100 g / 4 oz butter, softened
generous pinch of cayenne pepper
generous pinch of white pepper
1.25 ml / ¼ tsp curry powder
1.25 ml / ¼ tsp ground ginger

Beat all the ingredients together in a small bowl, using the back of the spoon to combine them thoroughly. Check the seasoning. Use at once or press into small pots, tapping the pots while filling to knock out all the air. Cover with foil and refrigerate until required. Use within 2 days.

MAKES 100 G / 4 OZ

LEMON AND HERB STUFFING

50 g / 2 oz butter
100 g / 4 oz fresh white breadcrumbs
30 ml / 2 tbsp chopped parsley
2.5 ml / ½ tsp chopped fresh thyme
grated rind of ½ lemon
salt and pepper

Melt the butter in a small saucepan. Add the breadcrumbs, herbs and lemon rind. Add salt and pepper to taste, then use as required.

SUFFICIENT FOR 8 (75 G / 3 OZ) THIN FISH FILLETS

SAGE AND ONION STUFFING

2 onions, thickly sliced
4 young fresh sage sprigs or 10 ml / 2 tsp dried sage
100 g / 4 oz fresh white breadcrumbs
50 g / 2 oz butter or margarine, melted
salt and pepper
1 egg, lightly beaten (optional)

Put the onions in a small saucepan with water to cover. Bring to the boil, cook for 2–3 minutes, then remove the onions from the pan with a slotted spoon. Chop them finely. Chop the sage leaves finely, discarding any stalk.

Combine the breadcrumbs, onions and sage in a bowl. Add the melted butter or margarine, with salt and pepper to taste. Mix well. If the stuffing is to be shaped into balls, bind it with the beaten egg.

SUFFICIENT FOR 1 (2.5 KG / 5½ LB) DUCK;
DOUBLE THE QUANTITY FOR 1 (4–5 KG / 9–11 LB) GOOSE

WHITE SAUCE

The recipe that follows is for a thick coating sauce. See below for variations.

50 g / 2 oz butter
50 g / 2 oz plain flour
600 ml / 1 pint milk, stock or a mixture
salt and pepper

Melt the butter in a saucepan. Stir in the flour and cook over low heat for 2–3 minutes, without browning.

With the heat on the lowest setting, gradually add the liquid, stirring constantly. If lumps begin to form, stop pouring in liquid and stir the sauce vigorously, then continue pouring in the liquid when smooth. Increase the heat to moderate and cook the sauce, stirring, until it boils and thickens.

Lower the heat and simmer for 1–2 minutes, beating briskly to give the sauce a gloss. Add salt and pepper to taste.

MAKES 600 ML / 1 PINT

VARIATIONS

- **Pouring Sauce** Follow the recipe above, but use only 40 g / 1½ oz each of butter and flour. Add one of the ingredients shown to the basic recipe, when the sauce is cooked:
  100 g grated cheese (cheddar);
  3–4 eggs, hard-boiled and chopped;
  60 ml / 4 tbsp parsley, chopped;
  175 g / 6 oz mushrooms, sliced and cooked in butter;
  45–60 ml / 3–4 tbsp mustard, made mild.

HOLLANDAISE SAUCE

This is the classic sauce to serve with poached salmon or other firm fish.

45 ml / 3 tbsp white wine vinegar
6 peppercorns
bay leaf
1 blade of mace
3 egg yolks
100 g / 4 oz butter, softened
salt and pepper

Combine the vinegar, peppercorns, bay leaf and mace in a small saucepan. Boil rapidly until the liquid is reduced to 15 ml / 1 tbsp. Strain into a heatproof bowl and leave to cool.

Add the egg yolks and a nut of butter to the vinegar and place over a pan of gently simmering water. Heat the mixture gently, beating constantly until thick. Do not allow it to approach boiling point.

Add the remaining butter, a little at a time beating well after each addition. When all the butter has been added the sauce should be thick and glossy. If the sauce curdles, whisk in 10 ml / 2 tsp cold water. If this fails to bind it, put an egg yolk in a clean bowl and beat in the sauce gradually. Add a little salt and pepper and serve the sauce lukewarm.

MAKES ABOUT 125 ML / 4 FL OZ

MICROWAVE TIP

Combine 30 ml / 2 tbsp lemon juice with 15 ml / 1 tbsp water in a large bowl. Add a little salt and white pepper and cook on High for 3–6 minutes or until the mixture is reduced by about two-thirds. Meanwhile place 100 g / 4 oz butter in a measuring jug. Remove the bowl of lemon juice from the microwave oven, replacing it with the jug of butter. Heat the butter on High for 2½ minutes. Meanwhile add 2 large egg yolks to the lemon juice, whisking constantly. When the butter is hot, add it in the same way. Return the sauce to the microwave oven. Cook on High for 30 seconds, whisk once more and serve.

BECHAMEL SAUCE

*Marquis Louis de Béchameil is credited with inventing
this French foundation sauce. For a slightly less rich version,
use half pale chicken or vegetable stock and half milk.*

**1 small onion, thickly sliced
1 small carrot, sliced
1 small celery stick, sliced
600 ml / 1 pint milk
1 bay leaf
few parsley stalks
1 fresh thyme sprig
1 clove
6 white peppercorns
1 blade of mace
salt
50 g / 2 oz butter
50 g / 2 oz plain flour
60 ml / 4 tbsp single cream (optional)**

Combine the onion, carrot, celery and milk in a saucepan. Add the herbs and spices, with salt to taste. Heat to simmering point, cover, turn off the heat and allow to stand for 30 minutes to infuse, then strain.

Melt the butter in a saucepan. Stir in the flour and cook over low heat for 2–3 minutes, without browning. With the heat on the lowest setting, gradually add the flavoured milk, stirring constantly.

Increase the heat to moderate, stirring until the mixture boils and thickens to a coating consistency. Lower the heat when the mixture boils and simmer the sauce for 1–2 minutes, beating briskly to give the sauce a gloss. Stir in the cream, if used, and remove the sauce from the heat at once. Do not allow the sauce to come to the boil again. Add salt if required.

MAKES ABOUT 600 ML / 1 PINT

BEARNAISE SAUCE

The classic accompaniment to grilled beef steak.
Béarnaise Sauce is also delicious with vegetables such as broccoli.

60 ml / 4 tbsp white wine vinegar
15 ml / 1 tbsp chopped shallot
5 black peppercorns, lightly crushed
1 bay leaf
2 fresh tarragon stalks, chopped, or 1.25 ml / ¼ tsp dried tarragon
1.25 ml / ¼ tsp dried thyme
2 egg yolks
100 g / 4 oz butter, cut into small pieces
salt and pepper

Combine the vinegar, shallot, peppercorns and herbs in a small saucepan. Boil until the liquid is reduced to 15 ml / 1 tbsp, then strain into a heatproof bowl. Cool, then stir in the egg yolks.

Place the bowl over a saucepan of simmering water and whisk until the eggs start to thicken. Gradually add the butter, whisking after each addition, until the sauce is thick and creamy. Add salt and pepper to taste.

MAKES ABOUT 175 ML / 6 FL OZ

BREAD SAUCE

600 ml / 1 pint milk
1 large onion studded with 6 cloves
1 blade of mace
4 peppercorns
1 allspice berry
1 bay leaf
100 g / 4 oz fine fresh white breadcrumbs
15 ml / 1 tbsp butter
salt and pepper
freshly grated nutmeg
30 ml / 2 tbsp single cream (optional)

Put the milk in a small saucepan with the studded onion, mace, peppercorns, allspice and bay leaf. Bring very slowly to boiling point, then remove from the heat, cover the pan and set it aside for 30 minutes.

Strain the flavoured milk into a heatproof bowl, pressing the onion against the sides of the strainer to extract as much of the liquid as possible. Stir in the breadcrumbs and butter, with salt, pepper and nutmeg to taste.

Set the bowl over simmering water and cook for 20 minutes, stirring occasionally until thick and creamy. Stir in the cream, if using, just before serving.

MAKES ABOUT 250 ML / 8 FL OZ

MICROWAVE TIP

There is no need to infuse the onion in the milk if the sauce is to be made in the microwave. Simply put the clove-studded onion in a deep bowl, cover and cook on High for 2 minutes. Add the spices, bay leaf and milk, cover loosely and cook on High for 6–6½ minutes. Stir in the remaining ingredients, except the cream, and cook for 2 minutes more. Remove the studded onion, whole spices and bay leaf. Whisk the sauce, adding the cream if liked.

BUTTER SAUCE

*This classic sauce, rich in the use of butter, is delicious
with plain, lightly poached white fish or some shellfish. For example,
serve with fresh cod, rolled plaice fillets or poached scallops. It is a
last minute sauce – make it only when you are ready to serve it.*

30 ml / 2 tbsp finely chopped onion or shallot
30 ml / 2 tbsp white wine vinegar
225 g / 8 oz unsalted butter, chilled
salt and white pepper
lemon juice

Place the onion or shallot and vinegar in a saucepan. Add 45 ml / 3 tbsp water
and bring to the boil. Boil until the liquid is reduced by half.

Meanwhile, cut the butter into chunks. Reduce the heat to the lowest setting so
that the liquid is below simmering point. Whisking constantly, add a piece of
butter. Continue adding the butter, one piece at a time, whisking to melt each
piece before adding the next.

The sauce should be pale, creamy in appearance and slightly thickened – rather
like single cream. Take care not to let the mixture become too hot or it will curdle.

Remove the pan from the heat when all the butter has been incorporated. Taste
the sauce, then add salt, white pepper and lemon juice to taste. Serve at once
with poached fish.

MAKES ABOUT 250 ML / 8 FL OZ

FRESH TOMATO SAUCE

Fresh tomato sauce has a multitude of uses in savoury cookery. It is one of the simplest accompaniments for plain cooked pasta, it is included in many baked dishes and it is, of course, excellent with grilled fish, poultry and meat.

30 ml / 2 tbsp olive oil
1 onion, finely chopped
1 garlic clove, crushed
1 bay leaf
1 rindless streaky bacon rasher, chopped
800 g / 1¾ lb tomatoes, peeled and chopped
60 ml / 4 tbsp stock or red wine
salt and pepper
generous pinch of sugar
15 ml / 1 tbsp chopped fresh basil or 5 ml / 1 tsp dried basil

Heat the oil in a saucepan and fry the onion, garlic, bay leaf and bacon over gentle heat for 15 minutes.

Stir in the remaining ingredients except the basil. Heat until bubbling, then cover the pan and simmer gently for 30 minutes or until the tomatoes are reduced to a pulp.

Rub the sauce through a sieve into a clean saucepan or purée in a blender or food processor until smooth, then rub it through a sieve to remove seeds, if required.

Reheat the sauce. Add the basil. Add more salt and pepper if required before serving.

MAKES ABOUT 600 ML / 1 PINT

BARBECUE SAUCE

This is a very adaptable sauce. It can be used as a marinade, as a basting sauce for chicken portions, steaks, chops and similar foods being cooked on the barbecue grill, or as a side sauce to serve with grilled meats.

30 ml / 2 tbsp oil
1 onion, finely chopped
2 garlic cloves, crushed
1 (397 g / 14 oz) can chopped tomatoes
45 ml / 3 tbsp red wine vinegar
30 ml / 2 tbsp soft dark brown sugar
30 ml / 2 tbsp tomato ketchup
10 ml / 2 tsp soy sauce
10 ml / 2 tsp Worcestershire sauce
salt and pepper

Heat the oil in a saucepan. Add the onion and garlic and fry over gentle heat for 4–6 minutes, until the onion is soft but not coloured. Stir in the remaining ingredients and bring to the boil. Lower the heat and simmer for 30–45 minutes, until the sauce is thick and well flavoured.

MAKES ABOUT 150 ML / ¼ PINT

GRAVY

giblets, carcass bones or trimmings from meat, poultry or game
1 bay leaf
1 thyme sprig
1 clove
6 black peppercorns
1 onion, sliced
pan juices from roasting (see Mrs Beeton's Tip)
25 g / 1 oz plain flour (optional)
salt and pepper

Place the giblets, bones, carcass and/or trimmings (for example wing ends) in a saucepan. Pour in water to cover, then add the bay leaf, thyme, clove, peppercorns and onion. Bring to the boil and skim off any scum, then lower the heat, cover the pan and simmer for about 1 hour.

Strain the stock and measure it. You need about 600–750 ml / 1–1¼ pints to make gravy for up to six servings. If necessary, pour the stock back into the saucepan and boil until reduced.

Pour off most of the fat from the roasting tin, leaving a thin layer and all the cooking juices. Place the tin over moderate heat; add the flour if the gravy is to be thickened. Cook the flour, stirring all the time and scraping all the sediment off the tin, for about 3 minutes, until it is browned. If the gravy is not thickened, pour in about 300 ml / ½ pint of the stock and boil, stirring and scraping, until the sediment on the base of the tin is incorporated.

Slowly pour in the stock (or the remaining stock, if making thin gravy), stirring all the time. Bring to the boil and cook for 2–3 minutes to reduce the gravy and concentrate the flavour slightly. Taste and add more salt and pepper if required.

SERVES FOUR TO SIX

MRS BEETON'S TIP

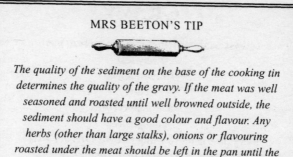

The quality of the sediment on the base of the cooking tin determines the quality of the gravy. If the meat was well seasoned and roasted until well browned outside, the sediment should have a good colour and flavour. Any herbs (other than large stalks), onions or flavouring roasted under the meat should be left in the pan until the gravy is boiled, then strained out before serving.

GRAVY NOTES

- If making gravy for a meal other than a roast, for example to accompany sausages or toad-in-the-hole, use a little fat instead of the pan juices and brown the flour well over low to moderate heat. Meat dripping gives the best flavour but butter or other fat may be used.
- To make onion gravy, slowly brown 2 thinly sliced onions in the fat before adding the flour – this is excellent with grilled sausages or toad-in-the-hole.
- Gravy browning may be added if necessary; however, it can make the sauce look artificial and unpleasant. Pale gravy is perfectly acceptable, provided it has good flavour.
- Always taste gravy when cooked. It should be well seasoned. If it lacks flavour, or is rather dull, a dash of Worcestershire sauce, mushroom ketchup or about 5–15 ml / 1–3 tsp tomato purée may be whisked in.
- Gravy may be enriched by adding up to half wine instead of stock.
- Add 60 ml / 4 tbsp port or sherry, and 15 ml / 1 tbsp redcurrant jelly to make a rich gravy for duck, game, lamb, pork or venison.
- Add 2 chopped pickled walnuts and 15 ml / 1 tbsp walnut oil to the pan juices to make a delicious walnut gravy.
- Use vegetable stock to make vegetable gravy. Cook a finely diced carrot and 2 thinly sliced onions in butter or margarine instead of using meat juices. Add 1.25 ml / ¼ tsp ground mace and 30 ml / 2 tbsp chopped parsley.
- Add 100 g / 4 oz thinly sliced mushrooms to the pan juices to make a mushroom gravy. The sauce may be further enriched by adding a little mushroom ketchup.

APPLE SAUCE

450 g / 1 lb apples
4 cloves
15 g / ½ oz butter
rind and juice of ½ lemon
sugar (see method)

Peel, core and slice the apples. Put them in a saucepan with 30 ml / 2 tbsp water, add the cloves, butter and lemon rind. Cover and cook over low heat until the apple is reduced to a pulp. Remove the cloves. Beat until smooth, rub through a sieve or process in a blender or food processor. Return the sauce to the clean pan, stir in the lemon juice and add sugar to taste. Reheat gently, stirring until the sugar has dissolved. Serve hot or cold.

MAKES ABOUT 350 ML / 12 FL OZ

CRANBERRY SAUCE

150 g / 5 oz sugar
225 g / 8 oz cranberries

Put the sugar in a heavy-bottomed saucepan Add 125 ml / 4 fl oz water. Stir over gentle heat until the sugar dissolves. Add the cranberries and cook gently for about 10 minutes until they have burst and are quite tender. Leave to cool.

MAKES ABOUT 300 ML / ½ PINT

VARIATIONS

- **Cranberry and Apple** Use half cranberries and half tart cooking apples.
- **Cranberry and Orange** Use orange juice instead of water. Add 10 ml / 2 tsp finely grated orange rind.

MAYONNAISE

Buy eggs from a reputable supplier and make sure they are perfectly fresh. Immediately before using wash the eggs in cold water and dry them on absorbent kitchen paper.

2 egg yolks
salt and pepper
5 ml / 1 tsp caster sugar
5 ml / 1 tsp Dijon mustard
about 30 ml / 2 tbsp lemon juice
250 ml / 8 fl oz oil (olive oil or a mixture of olive and grapeseed or sunflower oil)

Place the egg yolks in a medium bowl. Add salt and pepper, sugar, mustard and 15 ml / 1 tbsp of the lemon juice. Whisk thoroughly until the sugar has dissolved. An electric whisk is best; or use a wire whisk and work vigorously.

Whisking all the time, add the oil drop by drop so that it forms an emulsion with the egg yolks. As the oil is incorporated, and the mixture begins to turn pale, it may be added in a slow trickle. If the oil is added too quickly before it begins to combine with the eggs, the sauce will curdle.

The mayonnaise may be made in a blender or food processor. The egg mixture should be processed first, with 10 ml / 2 tsp of the oil added right at the beginning. With the machine running, add the rest of the oil drop by drop at first, then in a trickle as above.

When all the oil has been incorporated the mayonnaise should be thick and pale. Taste the mixture, then stir in more lemon juice, salt and pepper, if necessary. Keep mayonnaise in a covered container in the refrigerator for up to 5 days.

MAKES ABOUT 300 ML / ½ PINT

VARIATIONS

- **Aïoli** (good with fresh vegetable crudités) Add 2 fresh large crushed garlic cloves to the yolks with the seasonings.
- **Rouille** (good in soups) Add 2 fresh large crushed garlic cloves to the yolks. Omit the mustard. Add 15 ml / 1 tbsp paprika and 1.25 ml / ¼ tsp cayenne pepper to the yolk mixture before incorporating the oil

Useful Weights and Measures

USING METRIC OR IMPERIAL MEASURES

Throughout the book, all weights and measures are given first in metric, then in Imperial. For example 100 g / 4 oz, 150 ml/ ¼ pint or 15 ml / 1 tbsp.

When following any of the recipes use either metric or imperial – do not combine the two sets of measures as they are not interchangeable.

EQUIVALENT METRIC / IMPERIAL MEASURES

Weights The following chart lists some of the metric / imperial weights that are used in the recipes.

METRIC	IMPERIAL	METRIC	IMPERIAL
15 g	½ oz	375 g	13 oz
25 g	1 oz	400 g	14 oz
50 g	2 oz	425 g	15 oz
75 g	3 oz	450 g	1 lb
100 g	4 oz	575 g	1¼ lb
150 g	5 oz	675 g	1½ lb
175 g	6 oz	800 g	1¾ lb
200 g	7 oz	900 g	2 lb
225 g	8 oz	1 kg	2¼ lb
250 g	9 oz	1.4 kg	3 lb
275 g	10 oz	1.6 kg	3½ lb
300 g	11 oz	1.8 kg	4 lb
350 g	12 oz	2.25 kg	5 lb

Liquid Measures The following chart lists some metric/Imperial equivalents for liquids. Millilitres (ml), litres and fluid ounces (fl oz) or pints are used throughout.

METRIC	IMPERIAL
50 ml	2 fl oz
125 ml	4 fl oz
150 ml	¼ pint
300 ml	½ pint
450 ml	¾ pint
600 ml	1 pint

Spoon Measures Both metric and Imperial equivalents are given for all spoon measures, expressed as millilitres and teaspoons (tsp) or tablespoons (tbsp).

All spoon measures refer to British standard measuring spoons and the quantities given are always for level spoons.

Do not use ordinary kitchen cutlery instead of proper measuring spoons as they will hold quite different quantities.

METRIC	IMPERIAL
1.25 ml	¼ tsp
2.5 ml	½ tsp
5 ml	1 tsp
15 ml	1 tbsp

Length All linear measures are expressed in millimetres (mm), centimetres (cm) or metres (m) and inches or feet. The following list gives examples of typical conversions.

METRIC	IMPERIAL
5 mm	¼ inch
1 cm	½ inch
2.5 cm	1 inch
5 cm	2 inches
15 cm	6 inches
30 cm	12 inches (1 foot)

MICROWAVE INFORMATION

Occasional microwave hints and instructions are included for certain recipes, as appropriate. The information given is for microwave ovens rated at 650–700 watts.

The following terms have been used for the microwave settings: High, Medium, Defrost and Low. For each setting, the power input is as follows: High = 100% power, Medium = 50% power, Defrost = 30% power and Low = 20% power.

All microwave notes and timings are for guidance only: always read and follow the manufacturer's instructions for your particular appliance. Remember to avoid putting any metal in the microwave and never operate the microwave empty.

OVEN TEMPERATURES

Whenever the oven is used, the required setting is given as three alternatives: degrees Celsius (°C), degrees Fahrenheit (°F) and gas.

The temperature settings given are for conventional ovens. If you have a fan oven, adjust the temperature according to the manufacturer's instructions.

°C	°F	GAS
110	225	¼
120	250	½
140	275	1
150	300	2
160	325	3
180	350	4
190	375	5
200	400	6
220	425	7
230	450	8
240	475	9

Index